Sophocles: Oedipus at Colonus

DUCKWORTH COMPANIONS
TO GREEK AND ROMAN TRAGEDY

Series editor: Thomas Harrison

Aeschylus: Agamemnon Barbara Goward
Aeschylus: Eumenides Robin Mitchell-Boyask
Aeschylus: Persians David Rosenbloom
Aeschylus: Seven Against Thebes Isabelle Torrance
Euripides: Bacchae Sophie Mills
Euripides: Heracles Emma Griffiths
Euripides: Hippolytus Sophie Mills
Euripides: Ion Laura Swift
Euripides: Iphigenia at Aulis Pantelis Michelakis
Euripides: Medea William Allen
Euripides: Orestes Matthew Wright
Euripides: Phoenician Women Thalia Papadopoulou
Euripides: Suppliant Women Ian C. Storey
Euripides: Trojan Women Barbara Goff
Seneca: Phaedra Roland Mayer
Seneca: Thyestes P.J. Davis
Sophocles: Ajax Jon Hesk
Sophocles: Electra Michael Lloyd
Sophocles: Oedipus at Colonus Adrian Kelly
Sophocles: Philoctetes Hanna Roisman
Sophocles: Women of Trachis Brad Levett

DUCKWORTH COMPANIONS
TO GREEK AND ROMAN TRAGEDY

Sophocles:
Oedipus at Colonus

Adrian Kelly

Duckworth

First published in 2009 by
Gerald Duckworth & Co. Ltd.
90-93 Cowcross Street, London EC1M 6BF
Tel: 020 7490 7300
Fax: 020 7490 0080
info@duckworth-publishers.co.uk
www.ducknet.co.uk

A catalogue record for this book is available
from the British Library

ISBN 978 0 7156 3713 5

Typeset by Ray Davies
Printed and bound in Great Britain by
CPI Antony Rowe, Chippenham and Eastbourne

Contents

5

Meiner kleinen Maus

Acknowledgements

I should like to thank Tom Harrison, the editor of this series, for suggesting that I write on the *OC*, Bill Allan for his constant encouragement and advice on this project, and Deborah Blake for her copy-editing, managing and invaluable all-round help with the MS. Pat Easterling was extremely generous with her time, attention and offprints, and saved me from many infelicities of thought and expression. I should also like to thank the Alexander von Humboldt-Stiftung for a Forschungsstipendium in 2007-8, during which period the book was written, when Wolfgang Roesler, Friederike Herklotz and everyone at the Institut für Klassische Philologie at the Humboldt-Universität zu Berlin provided every form of support and advice. The Department of Classics and Ancient History at the University of Warwick generously gave me the research leave which enabled me to spend 2007-8 in Berlin, where the staff of both the Staatsbibliothek (Potsdamer Straße) and the Philologische Bibliothek of the Freie Universität were efficient, patient and good humoured with my poor German. Café Bondi in Schlegelstraße afforded the best coffee and worst banter in continental Europe, while there is presumably no need to specify the benefits to be derived from Sir Simon Rattle and the Berlin Philharmonic, or Daniel Barenboim and the Staatsoper Unter den Linden. Upon my return to the United Kingdom, my Balliol students and colleagues (Penny Bulloch, Bob Cowan, Jessica Moss and Rosalind Thomas) were both welcoming and stimulating. I thank also the following individuals, whose assistance was of various sorts, but great importance: Shy Abady, Tim Duff, Patrick Finglass, Shai Lavi, and the Seifert family.

Finally, thanks and love to my wife, Sophie Gibson, for putting up with me and the extra childcare duties engendered

Acknowledgements

by the writing of this book; and to the object of that care (and the book's dedicate), Matilda Kate Kelly, who was born in Berlin and provided a constant, and ever welcome, source of distraction.

Berlin, August 2008 / Oxford, August 2009

1

Sophocles and Athens

This first chapter aims to set out (1) the personal, (2) historical, (3) festival and (4) socio-political contexts for the *OC*, before we turn to detailed discussion of the play itself.

1. Sophocles

The sources for Sophocles' life are notoriously unreliable.[1] Summarised, bowdlerised, extrapolated from his own plays and others' (particularly the comedian Aristophanes), this material must be treated carefully and sceptically, though it would be unwise to use any such information to interpret the *OC* itself, e.g. in explaining its 'episodic' structure as the work of a tired old man.[2] However, one should not entirely dismiss unreliable or even obviously fictive stories, for they reveal how later ancient audiences interpreted Sophocles' works.[3]

As one of the three great tragic poets of antiquity, Sophocles attracted interest in every period, from the earliest references in Aristophanes (Radt, 'Testimonia' (hereafter T) 101-104d) or Ion of Chios (T 75) (fifth century BC) to the Byzantine lexicon, the *Suda* (T 2) (tenth century AD). A number of specialist works were devoted to the playwright, pre-eminent among them the important Hellenistic *Life* (T 1),[4] and another fruitful source are the *scholia* (marginal notes) derived from the works of ancient commentators and scholars, and transmitted with the medieval MSS of Sophocles and a range of other ancient authors. Some of the most interesting details come as random anecdotes in a range of authors from Aristotle and Plato (fourth century BC) to Eustathius (twelfth century AD).[5]

This wealth of interest produced its own problems. As one example, consider the connection between Sophocles' generalship in the war against Samos (441/0 BC) and his play *Antigone*,

a link first made in its ancient 'hypothesis' (summaries transmitted in the MSS for some plays, generally dated to the
Hellenistic period and later) (T 25): there it is suggested that
Sophocles won the office 'because of the [play's] high reputation'. Other narratives make it clear that the story's basis was
neither uncontested nor certain: the *Life* quotes Satyrus (third
century BC) for the story that Sophocles died from overexertion
in reciting the play (T 1.58-61) and compares that to the version
of 'others', that Sophocles died when he had heard that he had
won the competition with the production including the *Antigone*
(T 1.61-3). Death through joy is a prominent theme in later
stories of his passing, though the *Antigone* is not specifically
named as the play involved (T 85-7), while the other major
tradition about his death has him choking on a grape (T 88-90).
The biographical tradition was never smooth; there was no
single version of his life, and no narrative should be read as the
authoritative one. With this in mind, let us now turn to a few
basic 'facts' for Sophocles' life:

[1] born 496/5 [T 3, 33]
[2] died 406/5 [T 3]
[3] son of Sophillus [T 1.1; 7-11b]
[4] of the deme[6] Colonus [T 1.9-10, 2.1, 12-14 etc.]
[5] aristocrat [T 1.1-11]
[6] father of tragedian Iophon[7] [T 1.48, 2.8, 16, 17].

The first two items are contested, with several alternative dates
for both his birth (495/4 BC [T 1]; 488-485 BC [T 2]) and death
(408 BC [T 6a]; 411/0 BC [T 6b]; 403 BC [T 6c]), but all the sources
agree in making him very long lived. His father's and son's
names are not contested; the former's status is usually stated
as aristocratic (T 1.10, 15), while Sophocles' membership of the
deme Colonus, which was a settlement a little over a mile
north-west of Athens, is confirmed by an extant fifth-century BC
source (T 18): an entry in the Athenian tribute lists (tablets
listing the members of the Delian league and their tribute)
names 'Sophocles of Colonus' an *Hellênotamiâs* (treasurer of
the league).
    That Sophocles should have held public office is unsurpris-
ing, for citizens were expected to take part in Athens' political
life. As Thucydides has Pericles say in the famous Funeral

10

1. Sophocles and Athens

Speech (dramatic date 431 BC) 'we alone [the Athenians] consider a man who takes no part in [the state] not a private man (*apragmona*) but a useless one (*akhreion*)' (2.40.2). Several such offices are mentioned: Sophocles is constantly linked with a generalship (an important institution in Athens, comprising ten elected men in command of the army and navy during their year of office) in 441 BC (T 1.4, 1.35, 15.4, 19-25, 74a-d, 75.28-9, 104c.2), and perhaps another in 438 or 429 BC (T 1.35-6, 26).[8] He was also associated with the *probouloi* ('councillors') appointed after the Sicilian disaster in 413 BC and involved in the oligarchic revolution of 411 BC: Aristotle (*Rhetoric* 1419a25 = T 27) presents Sophocles as agreeing reluctantly, along with the other *probouloi*, to the establishment of the Four Hundred (new executive council replacing the more representative *boulê*).[9] Political participation entailed risks and, like many other office-holders and prominent citizens, Sophocles was subject to an Aristophanic barb: in *Peace* (421 BC), the character Trygaeus says, rather cryptically, that 'for the sake of gain, [Sophocles] would sail on a wicker-mat' (*Peace* 695-6),[10] though such accusations were an essential part of Athenian political discourse,[11] and one should never swallow whole any comment made on the comic stage.[12]

Religion was similarly important in Athenian public life, and it is particularly well represented in Sophocles' biography. He was associated with the cult of the healing deity Asclepius (T 1.39, 67-73a, 174.12), though the stories of his reception of the god into Athens, for which he received the name 'Dexion' ('receiver') (T 69-71), may represent fictive extrapolations of the fact that he had written a *paiân* ('victory song') for the god (T 72-3 = *PMG* 737):[13] the prominence of the first-person in this poetry could readily produce stories about such an encounter.[14] Of course, that Sophocles was then worshipped as a cult-hero under this name is a natural concomitant of the embellishing process (T 1.11), though this cannot account for his association with the priesthood of (the otherwise unknown) Halon or Alon (T 1.39-40).[15] The antiquity of all these stories can be doubted; at most, we can be relatively certain that he was worshipped as a hero in Athens by the time of Ister (mid-third century BC) (T 1.74-5).[16] Though of varied quality and trustworthiness, the association between hero cult and Sophocles himself is obviously important for the *OC*, where Oedipus' heroisation is the end point of the drama, as it is with the main characters in

11

several of Sophocles' other plays, notably the *Ajax* (undated) and the *Philoctetes* (409 BC).[17]

However, before one interprets the *OC* as an expression of personal piety, or a desire to be heroised, we should remember that a persistent theme in ancient writing about Sophocles characterises this play as an *apologia pro vita sua*, e.g. in the story that he recited in court the first *stasimon* of the *OC*, the famous Ode to Colonus (668ff.), in order to defeat a charge of mental incompetence made by his son Iophon (T 1.50f., 81-4).[18] Though here the quality of Sophocles' poetry is proof of his capacity, the parallels between his situation and Oedipus' (apparently powerless old men with ungrateful sons, who prove their worth, one at Colonus, the other through an ode in praise of Colonus – Sophocles' own home town!), would have been grist to the mill of ancient biographism, and would have thus encouraged (if not entirely prompted) the depiction of the playwright as either a hero himself,[19] or as someone particularly interested in the religious life of the city.

If there is little factual truth here, we can still conclude that there was something in Sophocles' drama which allowed a belief that he was a pious and dutiful citizen. These 'religious' stories, however true a reflection of his life or personal practices and beliefs, point us towards an early reception of his drama, and their ultimate example comes in the story that Heracles appeared to the playwright in a dream (T 1.41-6), revealing the location of a golden crown which had been stolen from the Acropolis; on receiving a talent as a reward, Sophocles used it to dedicate a temple of 'Heracles Informer'.[20] As the author of the *Life* says, 'Sophocles was loved of the gods as no other'.

Once the association between work and author had been made, the rest of the *OC* was ripe for this sort of reading: the antagonistic relationship between Oedipus and his son(s) could easily have given rise to the trial story (T 81-84a), particularly considering that Sophocles competed with his own son in the tragic festivals (T 1.78-9), and was perhaps *beaten* by him (T 64). Certainly some type of link is assumed in Aristophanes' *Frogs* (405 BC), when 'Dionysus' comments that it was too early to tell how good Iophon was, so soon after his father's death (*Frogs* 72-82 = T 101). Though this joke implies that Sophocles was writing or influencing his son's work, it still makes the point that an artistic relationship could be biographically interpreted, at least in a comic context; Richard Jebb plausibly argued that some type of contest between Sophocles and his son(s) was the subject of its own comedy.[21] Other sources accuse Iophon of passing off his father's work as his own (T 63), working with him (T 66), or even being responsible for some of Sophocles' plays (T 160). But no source is earlier than Aristophanes, and several (T 63-5) are mere explanations of his joke, so these later statements of Iophon's dependence on his father may go back no further than the *Frogs*.

This brings us to the strand of Sophocles' ancient biography most relevant for present purposes – his tragic career. The number of his victories is variously recorded, from 18 in the *didascaliae* (records of productions in Athens, collected later by Aristotle)[22] and Diodorus (T 85.2) to 20 in the *Life* (T 1.33) and 24 in the *Suda* (T 2.10); whichever figure is correct, he was extraordinarily successful, if we remember that Euripides won only four times during his lifetime, and Aeschylus thirteen. Of course, he wrote more plays than either (*c.* 130[23] to *c.* 90 each) and so competed more times (*c.* 33 to *c.* 23 each), and his strike rate varies, according to the number of victories, from 73% (24 wins) to 61% (20) and finally 55% (18). Compare these figures with Aeschylus' 57% and Euripides' 17%, and it is an excellent record which chimes well with the *Life's* statement that he never came third (T 1.33-4).

If competitive success were not enough, Sophocles was also attributed with several innovations: the third actor (also attributed to Aeschylus; cf. T 96), scene painting (T 1.23, 95), increasing the chorus from 12 to 15 members (T 1.22-3),[24] and being the first poet not to perform in his own plays (T 1.21-2) – though there is also a tradition that he did act some of the time (T. 1. 24-5, 99b.2), and other stories make great play with his youthful artistic achievements (T 1.15-17), one of them even relating that, as a young man, he led the performance of the *paian* for the victory over the Persians at Salamis in 480 BC (T 1.17-19). Again, it is very difficult to separate truth from fiction, but these stories show that the historical figure's depiction could be influenced by assumptions either ultimately derived from, or at least not uninfluenced by, his work.

*

Sophocles the son of Sophillus, of the deme Colonus, was a celebrity figure in Athens, who participated fully in the civic, political and religious life of his community. He was long-lived by contemporary standards, by some way the most successful of his competitors, and it is not impossible that he was responsible for at least some developments in Athenian theatre. Beyond these 'facts', we can be sure that his plays provided fruitful material for later biographical narratives, filling in the framework of 'reliable' details (in a manner not inconsistent with those details) by providing a celebrity character to explain that body of work. His success as an artist was augmented by pleasing and interesting stories about the pleasantness of his character, his personal charm and piety, a legal conflict with his sons in which he was the wronged figure, and so on. But these stories say less about Sophocles as an historical figure than about an idealised 'author' whose views and personality could be distilled from the plays.

While this material will not be used here to interpret the *OC* itself, we should remember the place of the drama within its context, and within the lives of the citizens of Athens, of whom Sophocles was one of the most famous. How this context could illuminate the drama, or at least provide a framework for its interpretation, is explored in the rest of this chapter.

2. The historical context

Athenian tragedy was once linked with its immediate historical context in very specific ways: Euripides' *Trojan Women* (415 BC) was a comment on the Athenian sack of Melos earlier in that year,[25] Aeschylus' *Oresteia* (458 BC) primarily a political broadcast in favour of Ephialtes' reforms of the Areopagus council,[26] and Sophocles' *Philoctetes* (409 BC) had something to do with bringing Alcibiades back to Athens to help them win the Peloponnesian War.[27] While the pendulum may have swung away from historicist readings of this sort, we should not characterise the *OC* as a 'timeless work of art' with no allusion to 'anything in the time of the poet'.[28] Such a specific definition of the 'political' is now largely a thing of the past, though that has not made the relationship between politics and tragedy any less contentious. The argument of this book is that there is a necessary and fruitful link between tragedy and its context, but that

14

playwrights did not use the stage to make specific comment, constructing their characters and plots as thinly veiled avatars of prominent Athenian politicians and events. Nonetheless, a discussion of the historical context can help to provide a sense of the times through which Sophocles and his audiences lived, and which shaped their expectations of the world around them.

Before doing that, we need to admit that the date of the composition of the *OC* is totally uncertain – not unusually, for only the *Philoctetes* (409 BC) of Sophocles' other plays is securely dated. The *OC*'s second hypothesis (T 41) states that it was produced by the younger Sophocles in the archonship of Micon (402/1 BC),[29] but the playwright himself died a few years before that, in 406/5 BC. When did he write it? The history of the Peloponnesian War's last ten years may provide a clue, specifically with regard to the oligarchic revolution in Athens of 411 BC. Thucydides (8.67.2) tells us that the assembly was 'gathered' or 'shut in' (see Hornblower (2008) 949) to the precinct of Poseidon in Colonus by the leading oligarchs. Colonus was a natural and rather symbolic place for this type of gathering, since its cult of Poseidon *Hippios* ('of horses') was heavily associated with the aristocrat-dominated Athenian cavalry (*hippeis*).[30] Given Sophocles' association with the oligarchic constitution, Lewis Campbell contended that the play was supportive of the new regime, and composed in or shortly after 411 BC, but could not be performed until the general amnesty issued after the end of the regime of the Thirty Tyrants in autumn 403 BC.[31] The theory largely depends on interpreting the play in one of the directly 'political' manners mentioned above, yet its fragility can be seen in the fact that Lachmann supposed, because of the play's patriotic character, that it was composed before the Peloponnesian War.[32] Neither can be proved – or disproved, for that matter – but they show how specifically politicised interpretations can lead to two mutually exclusive, and equally plausible, positions.

Another clue has been seen in the *OC*'s enigmatic prediction of conflict between Thebes and Athens (409-11), and Oedipus' promise of aid, once more against the Thebans (616-23). Certainly the former passage (esp. 411 'when [the Thebans] stand by your tomb') looks on first sight very specific, and has been matched with Diodorus' story (13.72.3-73.1) of an engagement between Boeotian and Athenian cavalry (407 BC), or Xenophon's narrative (*Hellenica* 1.1.33) of an encounter with the Peloponnesians (410 BC). However promising these angles may seem, Diodorus nowhere mentions Colonus (though he does have the Spartan King Agis camp at the nearby Academy), nor does Xenophon speak specifically of Boeotians or cavalry involvement. Furthermore, the language of the prophecy need not refer to any single engagement, for the Greek is vague, could refer to a series of such occasions, and the uncertainty over the site of the tomb means that the prediction might refer to any Theban attack at all. The promise of generalised future aid to Athens against one's own countrymen is typical of such figures (e.g. Orestes in Aeschylus' *Eumenides* 767-74, Eurystheus in Euripides' *Children of Heracles* 1040-3).[33] In addition, cavalry skirmishes with Peloponnesian raiding parties or expeditions from Decelea (a settlement about 20 km north of Athens) were a common occurrence during this period (Thucydides (7.27.5) speaks of daily excursions by the Athenian *hippeis* towards Decelea),[34] so there is no reason to suppose that Sophocles and his audience would not have associated Oedipus' prediction with this *type* of encounter, but it cannot provide a secure date for the play's composition.

Taking a small leap in the dark, the current scholarly consensus looks to the period after the *Philoctetes* (409 BC).[35] On that basis, perhaps the required Athenian narrative is that of the years 411-406 BC: while short-lived, the oligarchic revolution in 411 BC showed how unstable Athenian politics had become after the disaster in Sicily in 413 BC, though the idea of a terminal crisis in Athenian life and morality – a commonplace in modern writing about the period – surely needs some modification. There is no doubt that Athens found itself under tremendous strain during this period, as allies and tribute states deserted or revolted from the Delian league one after the other, and were only slowly and partially brought back under control, while additional pressure was placed on the countryside by the Peloponnesians at Decelea (from which this phase of the war is usually named), whither slaves were deserting at an alarming rate. Nonetheless, the story is not one of continual defeat until the final catastrophe at Aegospotamoi (405 BC).

Indeed, even though Attica was under constant observation from Decelea, the countryside was not abandoned, and the

16

Athenian cavalry and other armed formations – not to mention their extensive system of forts – were constantly involved in keeping the enemy at bay in the hinterland. Victor Hanson has shown how estimates of the damage inflicted by the Peloponnesians at Decelea have been greatly exaggerated, and provides a picture of life in the countryside in this period quite at variance with the gloom usually offered (especially) by literary critics.[36] The major theatre of war had in fact passed to the Eastern Aegean, where the Spartans (with Persian gold) were threatening Athens' life-line to the grain supplies of the Black Sea. In a series of battles (Cynossema 411 BC, Abydus 410 BC, Cyzicus 410 BC, Arginusae 406 BC), however, the Athenians actually defeated Peloponnesian fleets, but the instabilities of domestic politics undermined their successes; after a loss at Notium in 406 BC, Alcibiades (reinstated in 411 BC) fell from favour once more and, when a storm prevented the retrieval of Athenian dead after Arginusae, the responsible generals were executed or banished. Finally, in 405 BC, the Spartan commander Lysander won a crushing victory at Aegospotamoi, catching most of the Athenian fleet on the shore, and effectively ending the war. Whether or not Athens' defeat was inevitable is an open question, but the military record shows that an expectation of defeat was by no means the only one possible for an Athenian citizen before Aegospotamoi.[37]

Internally, as the aftermath of Arginusae indicates, political life in Athens was conducted in an extraordinary, and not always harmonious, climate. Indeed, after that battle citizenship had been granted to slaves serving in the navy, an institution whose importance was even more underlined after the loss of Euboea (with its grain supply) in 411 BC. The tensions thus brought about, viz. an increased reliance on the navy for the survival of the city (for its protection of the grain shipping routes from the Black Sea), necessarily had an impact on the nature of Athenian politics.[38]

The second historical narrative surrounds the production of the play in 401 BC. After the end of the war, the Spartans had installed a regime which came to be known as the Thirty Tyrants; the name really says it all. Not at all lamented when they were overthrown by democrats under Thrasyboulus in 403 BC, their reign had been one of terror and violence, and its social ramifications were to affect Athenian political discourse for

17

many years. The restoration of the democracy came with an amnesty for activities on either side in the civil war which, though it did not herald the immediate end of social discord, provided the framework for the re-establishment of political normality in the city.[39] The events of these two periods are certainly part of the context in which the *OC* needs to be read, but the play as an artistic and dramatic whole should not be reduced to an apology either for the oligarchs in general or for Sophocles' participation in that movement in particular. Nor will it be seen as a reaction to a specific reversal or success in the last phase of the Peloponnesian War. After all, Sophocles intended to submit the play to his fellow citizens in a contest, looking for their approval and support, and seeking to say something meaningful to them about their past, present and future. To those citizens in 411-406 BC, facing the continuation of a long and difficult war with some measure of hope, but an abiding awareness of how tough it was going to be, the play presents a positive vision of Athens and its historical trajectory, moving its depiction beyond present difficulties to the promises and potentialities of past and future. This message would have resounded even more powerfully for the same citizens in 401 BC, as they were coming to terms with defeat and its aftermath, and looking for the reassurance which the *OC*'s larger view of Athens provides. But first we shall have to see what the festival context tells us about the social and political import of Athenian tragedy.

3. The festival context

The performance of tragedy in Athens during the fifth century BC was pre-eminently staged at the 'City Dionysia', a five-day festival held during the month of Elaphebolion ('deer-hunt'; late March-early April).[40] The festival was preceded on the 8th of Elaphebolion by the *proagon* ('before-contest'), during which the playwrights would present their stories to the crowd. On the following day, Dionysus' cult statue was taken from his temple to the Academy (north-west environs of Athens, rather near Colonus) where the road from Eleutherai (small community on Attica's northern border) wound its way towards Athens, and then conducted into the city on the 10th of Elaphebolion in a procession re-enacting the 'original' arrival of Dionysus into the city. The three tragedians to compete had already been selected by the eponymous *arkhôn* (the 'magistrate' whose name was used to date the year) probably soon after taking up office in the previous summer,[41] and they were each given a day (12th-14th of the month) on which to present their tetralogy (three tragedies and a satyr play). Each day of the tragic performances conducted during the Peloponnesian War was probably concluded by a comedy (before and after that period an extra day was required to accommodate five comedies, but the order of events is unclear).[42]

Like all ancient Greek festivals, the City Dionysia was 'embedded' in its social context. Before the first tragedy, libations were poured by the ten generals of that year, the city's benefactors (citizens or not) were publicly rewarded, the tribute from Athens' allies in the Delian League was displayed before the audience, and the orphans of those citizens who had died fighting for their country (and whose rearing had been subsidised by the city) were presented with their first suit of armour. These were all highly visible symbols of Athens' power and prestige, and they were on show not only for citizens but also the many metics (*metoikoi* 'resident aliens'), allies and foreigners who came to view the magnificent spectacle on offer.

A range of ancient evidence attests to the festival's extravagance, for the Athenian rich competed with one another in the presentation of tragedies (and other choral performances), since they were responsible for paying for the costumes and training of the chorus (actors and poets were paid by the state).[43] This *khorêgia* ('duty of presenting a chorus') was one of the major ways in which the democratic city's elite could display their wealth. Athenian political discourse was extremely wary of the powerful individual, who could always be accused of trying to overturn the democracy and 'ostracised' from the community (the process takes its name from the pot-sherds (*ostraka*) on which the citizen would write (or have written for him) the name of the unwelcome individual, though the institution fell into general disuse in the latter part of the fifth century BC). In fact, 'putting on a chorus' was a 'liturgy' (*leitourgia*) which the rich were expected to perform, and which in turn provided the type of social cachet which could be called upon by someone in trouble as evidence of goodwill towards the community. The

19

worth of this particular favour can be illustrated by the fact that another (though more expensive) liturgy during this period of almost unremitting warfare was fitting out a trireme for the navy. Though Plutarch was exaggerating when he said that the Athenians spent more on these festivals than they did on their navy (*On the Glory of Athens* 348d-9b), the *polis* took this entertainment very seriously indeed.[44]

Yet the community's participation was not limited to the rich paying, or the ordinary citizens watching, or indeed in the city's provision of *honoraria* and prizes to the poets, and its payment of the actors, for citizens also served in the chorus.[45] The festival demanded the participation of Athenians from several social levels – as performers, spectators, and financiers – nor should we forget the overwhelming dominance of Athenians as authors of tragedy, which marks something of a contrast with the dithyrambic competition held at the Dionysia.[46] Finally, at the end of the festival, when the judges had reached their decision and awarded the prizes, an assembly was held in the theatre of Dionysus, and the conduct of the festival was debated.[47] So not only were the tragedies deeply Athenian in their personnel and presentation, but the whole process was closed by perhaps the most typically Athenian – and political – of all public gatherings.

It is therefore no surprise that 'politics' should have something to do with the interpretation of the plays themselves. Rightly so. Given Pericles' famous description of the Athenian citizen (quoted above, pp. 10-11), the common ancient characterisation of Athens as one of the most politically busy and energetic city-states, and the intensely political nature of Athenian comedy,[48] it would be strange if there were to be no link between the community and the themes explored in the high profile tragedies which dominated the festival. But how are these purposes to be evidenced in the tragedies themselves?

4. The socio-political context

One way has the poet making direct political comment. For instance, remembering that Sophocles died in 406 BC, and his involvement in the political revolution of 411 BC, Lowell Edmunds contended that the *OC* is a plea for unity and tolerance towards the *hippeis*, who had a leading role in that revolution, and who had a special association with the cult of Poseidon

Hippios in Colonus, Sophocles' own deme, where the first 'new' assembly in 411 BC had been called.[49] This links the poet, his own political 'misdemeanours' and the malodoured *hippeis* as essential to Athens' past and future greatness. The heavily pro-Athenian messages which the festival itself was giving to its audience are, on this reading, manipulated by Sophocles for his own defence, and that of a sizeable portion of his fellow citizens.

One can take precisely the opposite tack, with exactly the same material, and say that Sophocles was trying to criticise his fellow citizens, and to show them how far off track they had gone:[50] Theseus' Athens is a veiled reference to Pericles' Athens, which 'in name ... was a democracy, but actually it was the rule of one man' (Thucydides 2.65.10). As Thucydides argued in his epitaph (Pericles died from the plague in 429 BC, quite some time before the *OC*), the nature of politics subsequently became debased: there were no leaders, simply demagogues who pandered to the Athenian mob (2.65.7ff.). This massively oversimplified, but often repeated, description can be linked with the promise of Oedipus' aid for Athens, so long as it keeps the secret of his tomb safe, handed down from ruler to ruler (625-6, 1530-4).[51] This had failed to happen, for the system of responsible rule by the favoured one or few had been abandoned, and 'radical' Athens was now on the verge of being overwhelmed by the very Thebans (among others) against whose incursions the tomb of Oedipus was supposed to guard them. As with the arguments of Campbell and Lachmann, the same material can support opposite conclusions.

This is partially due to the rather intangible notion of 'high art', able to reach beyond its immediate context to those never imagined by the author or his original audiences. But both interpretations highlight only a few elements within the play, and therefore give an unbalanced impression of the drama as a whole. Indeed, there are good reasons to think that it was largely not the intention of Athenian playwrights to make such comments at all. There are, of course, some plays which do reference contemporary issues, and in some ways that is inevitable. After all, there is no point (perhaps no possibility of) retelling monarcho-aristocratic myths for an audience without including themes they found meaningful. Nonetheless, a 'direct' interpretation, which reads issues right off the stage into the

21

world of the audience, misses two very important points about Athenian tragedy.

The first is that, with very few exceptions, the playwrights avoided stories too close, spatially or temporally, to the world of their audience.[52] One reason they did this is suggested by Herodotus' story (6.21.2) of the early dramatist Phrynichus (active *c.* 511-476 BC).[53] He put on a drama (*c.* 492 BC) about the Persian capture of Miletus (*c.* 494 BC) during the failed Ionian revolt (an attempt in the first decade of the fifth century BC by the Greek cities of Asia Minor to free themselves from Persian overlordship). Phrynicus was fined because he reminded the Athenians too much of 'their own troubles'; being 'ethnically' related to the Ionians of Asia Minor (for Athens thought of itself as their mother city), and having failed to free them, the audience seems to have felt that this particular drama was simply too close to the bone – and perhaps a little foreboding, for the Persians would sack Athens itself in 480 BC. Both Herodotus' story and the plots of the plays seem to suggest that it was, or became, the norm to have distance, at least in setting, between the two worlds. The Athenians liked a bit of space between themselves and the suffering characters on stage.

The second reason is that, for all that the characters were human beings, with human concerns and faults, they existed in a world very different from that of the audience. The characters were the great figures of the very definite past which, whatever its similarities with the contemporary world, was in the end a rather different place – a place where gods routinely interacted with the major players, where violent death within the family at the hands of other family members was commonplace, where extremity of character and action defined the dynamics between the protagonists.

So there are boundaries between the worlds of the play and that of the audience. How to bridge them, indeed how the Athenian audience did so and understood the plays, is a point of great contention. The 'political' interpretations just mentioned use a one-to-one method: an allusion to Colonus must invoke contemporary events and associations of that place. Of course, it is not inconceivable that at least some of the audience might draw that conclusion. Thus Theseus becomes not just a paragon of responsible monarchy – something held in absolute abhorrence at Athens since the expulsion of their own tyrants, the sons of Peisistratus, at the end of the sixth century BC – but a good example of what the Athenians had lost in their version of 'mob rule'.[54]

An even more subtle version of this type of interpretation would hold that subversion, even downright criticism, of the Athenian *polis* was precisely the purpose of the dramas staged at the City Dionysia. According to this way of reading, both audiences and playwrights took part in a civic discourse which routinely challenged and questioned itself and the basic values of the *polis* – the primacy of the community, the subordination of the individual, the repression of women, and so on.[55] This would demand that, if someone on stage uses good rhetoric to a bad end, as Creon is often considered to do in his encounter with Oedipus (e.g. 761-2), then the playwright must be suggesting that speech – on which the Athenian state, in its assemblies and lawcourts, absolutely depended – is fundamentally dangerous. The subversive potential of Athenian tragedy thus becomes boundless: if something is wrong, e.g., with the Argive assembly in Euripides' *Orestes* (408 BC), then the same problems apply to the Athenian assembly; if Aphrodite is cruel in Euripides' *Hippolytus* (428 BC), there is something fundamentally awry with the nature of the divine, and so on.

But a number of considerations encourage us to think that the audiences looked on the dramas in a slightly different way. First, Plato writes in the fourth century BC of the audience in a manner suggesting that intelligent subversion was the last thing going on in the theatre; he criticises the poets for flattering and pandering to their audiences, not instructing them.[56] Secondly, the Theatre of Dionysus itself was large – the most recent estimates of its capacity range up to 7,000 people, roughly the size of the Pnyx, the area where the citizens assembled to debate and decide policy.[57] Although people had to pay a price of two *obols* to see the tragedies, the size of the place alone ensured that you could never be certain about just which particular group of citizens was going to dominate the cheering. And that brings us to the third point – competition. The poets were above all competing to win a prize, and one which relied in no small measure on the favourable reaction of the audience. How likely would it be for a poet, trying to win a competition judged by his fellow citizens, to put on a play which essentially told them that their political and social institutions were worthless? Perhaps in a modern, pluralistic context we can imagine such a figure, writing for a small public in small places; in the mass context of Athenian theatre, it is not quite so easy to do so.

A final way (my own, in fact) of bridging the gap is to argue that distance and difference were precisely the point.[58] The playwright wished to illustrate to his audience how and why they held the values they did – why extreme characters are worshipped in hero cult rather than given positions of political prominence (or perhaps why they should not be allowed those positions), why monarchical rule is so fraught with danger, why the passions of the individual need to be governed, and so on. But this makes the tragedian a somewhat sterile figure, pointedly lecturing his audience, and so I prefer to see this type of instruction as subsumed within the re-creation of heroic myth (concerned, after all, with great kings and heroes) for an Athenian audience living long after that heroic age, in a democratic society. Appealing to this group was the poet's business, and they were a varied bunch: aristocrats, democrats, citizens and metics across the social scale. This variety actively militated against tragedy's expression of what we would call propaganda, but it should not lead us away from audience values and expectations in heroic mythology, still less the poet's awareness and membership of the same system. On this reading, the *OC* looks to win the approval of its audience, and it does so (in part) by advancing a positive image of Athens – perhaps an ideal but an important one – as the shining example of *polis* civilisation, where the weak are protected and the virtuous rewarded. At the end of the play, Athens is to benefit from Oedipus' cult as a reward for its generosity and kindness; its fortune and reputation will shine into the future well beyond any single military threat or any defeat, for its greatness is sourced in heroic myth, and confined to no simple or single period of history.

*

So what can all these contexts tell us about tragedy in general, and the *OC* in particular? Performances were magnificent occasions, the festival and its ceremonies advertised Athenian supremacy and power, and the process was dominated by Athenian citizens, institutions and money. To be frank, the plays can be read against this background in almost any way – directly political (as Campbell, Lachmann, Kirkwood, Edmunds) and critical or supportive of Athens, or socio-political and subversive (as Goldhill), or socio-political and supportive (with Sourvinou-Inwood and Seaford). The flexibility of Athenian drama, its ability to live beyond a single reading, is one of the reasons it flourished elsewhere even in the fifth century BC.[59] Others included the beauty of its language, the tension of the action and its emotions, the richness of the costume, indeed the joy in theatrical experience, and so we must never interpret the plays only for what they reveal of Athenian social discourse. Sophocles' mastery of the entirety of the tragic art drove his massive success and contemporary celebrity. But ever present behind the individual *praxis* was an inherent distance and difference structuring the dynamic between the worlds of the play and its audience, creating interpretative room for other groups while constructing a generally affirmative message for its original one. Let us keep that original – Athenian – context ever before our eyes.

2

A Synopsis of the Play

Terms marked with an asterisk are defined in the *Metrical Appendix* at the end of this chapter.

In the fifth century BC theatre of Dionysus in Athens, the audience was faced with a dancing area (*orchêstra*), either circular or rectilinear, situated in front of an acting area.[1] It is entirely uncertain whether this area was raised or marked off at all from the *orchêstra*. Two entrance paths (*eisodoi*) branched out along either end, along which the actors and chorus enter and exit, with the path on the audience's left leading towards Thebes, that on the right in the direction of Athens.[2] Behind the acting area was a wooden hut (*skênê*), representing (the interior of) the grove of the Eumenides in Colonus. Despite the tradition that Sophocles was responsible for inventing '*skênê* painting' (T 95), we do not know whether this structure was painted, nor indeed what use was made of sets and scenery.[3] Aside from at least one stone seat in the acting area (19; cf. also 192-6),[4] there was a statue of the hero 'Colonus' himself ('they claim *this* horseman Colonus / as their leader' 59-60).

Prologos[5] (1-116)

Oedipus and Antigone enter (*from the audience's left*)[6] and, after an initial enquiry from the former which makes clear their identity and circumstance (1-13), Antigone leads him to rest on a rock (*acting area centre*). Following a short dialogue (14-27), Antigone announces the arrival of a stranger (28-32) (*audience right*). Addressed by Oedipus, the stranger at first demands Oedipus come out of the grove and, on his refusal, describes the sanctity and identity of the place, including information about Colonus and its political subordination to Athens (33-69). Oedipus begs him to

26

summon Theseus with an indeterminate promise of reward (70-4), but the stranger promises to inform the locals instead, departing (*audience right*) with an injunction to remain in the grove (75-80). The old man utters a prayer to the Eumenides for their support in fulfilling the oracle which Apollo had once given him, to the effect that his rest from care would come in a place dedicated to them (84-110). Antigone bids him be silent, since the men from Colonus (the chorus) are coming, and they retreat further into the grove (111-16) (*acting area front to rear, perhaps through the door of the skêné*).[7]

Parodos (117-253)

The chorus (old men of Colonus) enter (*from the right, heading into the orchestra*), in the process of searching for the stranger who has defiled the sacred place (first strophe* 118-37, generally sung in aeolic* rhythms). Oedipus reveals himself (*from the skêné*), to their horrified reaction (anapaestic* dialogue 138-48), though their full description of his pitiful appearance comes in their following song (first antistrophe* 150-69) before they bid him to come out of the grove. After further dialogue, this time with Antigone, Oedipus comes out of the sacred area (*acting area rear to front*), an action carried out during the last two (again basically aeolic*) strophic* pairs of the parodos (176-87 / 192-206/7) and its anapaestic* interlude between Antigone and Oedipus (188-91). Oedipus is guided to a stone seat (192-202),[8] and at the close of the second antistrophe* the chorus request Oedipus' identity, which he reveals reluctantly (207/8-36) in the (metrically mixed – aeolic*, anapaestic* and dactylic*) dialogic epode* (207/8-53). The information provokes another horrified reaction from the chorus and in return Antigone's supplication song (237-53).

First episode A (254-509)

After a brief choral statement of pity (254-7) in response to Antigone's supplication, Oedipus delivers a defence of his life and deeds (258-91), the final judgement on which the chorus defers to Theseus, who is already apparently on his way simply because of the rumour of Oedipus' presence (292-309). Antigone interrupts this exchange with the announcement of Ismene's approach (310-23) (*aud. left*), which is followed by a joyful

27

reunion between the three and Oedipus' thankful description of his daughters' services (324-60). Ismene brings the news of strife between Polyneices and Eteocles, the impending Argive attack on the city in support of the former's claims to the throne (361-84), as well as the import of a recent oracle that Oedipus' assistance is essential to success in the coming war. Consequently, she informs her father, Creon himself will try to persuade Oedipus to return with him, but with the important qualification that he should be settled not on Theban territory itself (385-415). Asking whether his sons know of the oracle (416-20), Oedipus curses them vehemently, recalling their earlier indifference to his fate and refusal to help him, before denying his aid to Thebes and offering it instead to Athens (421-60). The story has worked its effect on the chorus, who welcome Oedipus and instruct him to propitiate the Eumenides (461-92); he agrees, though Ismene is sent in his place because of his infirmity and blindness (493-509) (*exit into skênê*).[9]

Amoibaion (510-48)

In this short song dividing the first episode, the first strophic* pair (510-20 / 521-33) dominated by aeolic* rhythms, the second (534-41 / 542-8) by iambic,* a dialogue is conducted between Oedipus and the chorus, who ask pruriently for more information on his horrible past, which he eventually gives, closing again his account with a denial of his agency (539-41) resuming the theme of his first apology (258-91).

First episode B (549-667)

Theseus enters (*aud. right*) with an expression of support and pity for Oedipus' plight (551-68) and, in his following exchange with the blind old man (569-628), hears of the coming benefit which Oedipus is to bring, the eagerness of the Thebans to reclaim him, and the oracle about his death. Theseus accepts him under his protection and into the city (631-42) and, on hearing that Oedipus wishes to remain at Colonus (643-7), leaves the scene (*aud. right*) after reassuring him of his determination to keep his word and the old man safe (648-68).

First stasimon (668-719) – the 'Ode to Colonus'

A short stasimon, broken up into two strophic* pairs (668-80 / 681-93 and 694-706 / 707-719) dominated in turn by aeolic* and iambic* elements, delivers the famous encomium of Colonus and Attica. The first strophic* pair concentrates on the natural wonders of Colonus and its favouring by Dionysus, the Muses and Aphrodite; the second emphasises Attica more generally and its favour by Zeus, Athene and Poseidon, evinced in the olive tree granted by Athene, and Poseidon's gift of good horses and colts, along with the salt well-spring on the Acropolis, all gifts which promise martial success on both land and sea.

Second episode A (720-832)

As with the first episode, this is divided into two sections by a lyric dialogue in strophic* pairs (833-43 / 876-86). The first section (720-832) concerns the confrontation between Oedipus and Creon, the second (887-1043) that between Oedipus, Creon and the newly arrived Theseus. The first introduces Creon (and attendants) (*aud. left*), as he tries to persuade Oedipus to return to Thebes with him (728-60). Oedipus angrily refuses to go, accusing Creon of opportunism and hypocrisy (761-99) before their encounter degenerates into rapid-fire dialogue and threats (800-32). During its course Creon moves from not inapposite statements about Oedipus' rather intemperate character (800-12) to using the fact that he has seized Ismene – and will soon take Antigone – as an inducement for their father's acquiescence (813-21). Oedipus appeals to the chorus and they try (as usual, ineffectively) to prevent Creon, who proceeds to take hold of Antigone (822-32).

Amoibaion (833-86)

This attempt is then played out (*moving aud. left*) in the generally dochmiac* and iambic* strophe* (833-43) which opens with Oedipus calling on the city's help and closes with the chorus' cry to a similar end. A short iambic* passage (844-75) – parallel with the earlier exchange (800-32) after Creon's initial attempt at persuasion – has Antigone crying for help and Oedipus bewailing his weakness (844-7), before Creon rebukes him for his stubbornness and decides to seize the old man as well (848-75). Again the poet switches into (emotionally more elevated) song (876-86) to accompany the action, the antistrophe* detailing roughly the same interplay between Creon ('I will do this'), the chorus ('you'd better not') and Oedipus ('o wretch that I am').

Second episode B (887-1043)

The episode's second section now introduces Theseus (and attendants) (*aud. right*), who arrives from a sacrifice demanding to know the reason for all the shouting. Informed briefly by Oedipus (891-6), he swiftly gives orders for Creon's men to be pursued and Oedipus' children restored to him (897-904; 932-6), reproving Creon for his unseemly behaviour (905-31). Creon's reply begins with a claim that he was simply trying to remove an unholy creature from Attic land, as the Areopagus would have demanded (939-50), as well as excusing his action on the grounds that Oedipus had angered him (951-9). Instead of Theseus, Oedipus replies to Creon, delivering the third of his defence speeches in this play (960-1013). His grounds here are that he killed his father when he didn't know who he was and when the latter was trying to kill him, and that he married his mother unknowingly. He closes with a wish that Athens revenge itself suitably on Creon for his outrage (1003-13). The section closes with Theseus demanding the Theban lead him to the place where Creon's men are (1016-17 / 1019-35) and, though the latter murmurs darkly about the consequences of this action (1036-7), Theseus reassures Oedipus about the safe return of his daughters before departing in pursuit (1038-43) (*aud. left*).

Second stasimon (1044-95) –
the 'Battle Ode'

In a short song composed of two strophic* pairs (1044-58 / 1059-73 and 1074-84 / 1085-95), the first again basically aeolic* and iambic* in rhythm, the second more mixed (but frequently iambic*), the chorus imagine for the audience the clash between Theseus' band and Creon's, invoking the aid of Ares, Athene and Poseidon, as well as Zeus and Apollo.

Third episode (1096-1210)

The scene opens with the joyful return of Antigone and Ismene (*aud. left*) and their reunion with Oedipus (1099-1118).[10] He thanks the returned Theseus (1119-38), who replies in kind before alerting Oedipus to the presence of a stranger at the altar of Poseidon who asks simply to speak to him (1139-62); they puzzle over his identity for a while until Theseus reveals that the stranger has come from Argos (1163-7), whereon Oedipus identifies this new suppliant traveller as his son and refuses to speak with him despite Theseus' interjections (1168-80). Antigone pleads with her father to speak with Polyneices (1181-1203), and Oedipus relents, with an injunction that no one should remove him from Athens by force (1204-7). To this Theseus assents before departing (1208-10) (*aud. right*).

Third stasimon (1211-48)

Structured as a triad* (strophe* 1211-23 / antistrophe* 1224-38 / epode* 1239-48), this song is essentially gnomic in character (and aeolic* in rhythm), postulating the desirability of a short life given the troubles and toils which come upon men as they grow old. The chorus relate these explicitly to Oedipus (1239f.) as well as themselves, and close with a reflection on the many sources of *âtê* ('delusion' or 'affliction' more generally) which seem to have buffeted Oedipus throughout his life.

Fourth episode A (1249-1446)

As the scene opens, Polyneices enters (*aud. right*),[11] bewailing the miserable state of his father and sisters (1254-66), before detailing his determination to rectify matters (1267-70). At his father's silence, he turns to his sisters (1271-9) and, urged to speak at greater length by Antigone (1280-3), he begins his lengthy defence (1284-1345). His speech narrates his expulsion from Thebes at the hands of Eteocles (1292-1300) and subsequent enlistment of Argive allies (1301-25). He mentions the oracle predicting victory for those to whom Oedipus attaches himself (1326-32), begs him to aid them, and closes with an emotional appeal to his father – seeking to link them as fellow-exiles (1333-7) – and a promise to restore him to his household (1342-5).

Oedipus' reply begins inauspiciously, directed to the chorus and stating that it was only out of favour for Theseus that he suffered Polyneices to speak at all (1348-51). He then launches into a furious denunciation of his son, focusing (as in his reply to Creon in the second episode) on his hypocrisy in pushing Oedipus out of Thebes but only now remembering with shame his terrible plight (1354-64), and comparing his filial duty unfavourably with that of his daughters (1365-9). Oedipus predicts his sons' deaths in the coming battle, calling down curses to be witnessed by Tartarus, the Eumenides and Ares (1370-92). The chorus tersely bids Polyneices to leave (1397-8), at which he bewails the fate of his companions and begs his sisters to return home and care for his corpse (1399-1413). The scene closes with a pathetic dialogue between Polyneices and his sister (1414-46), in which Antigone tries unsuccessfully to dissuade him from returning to the Argive army before he leaves (*aud. left*).

Amoibaion (1447-1504)

Composed of two strophic* pairs in generally dochmiac* and iambic* rhythms (1447-56 / 1462-71 and 1477-85 / 1491-9), with each (anti)strophe* being separated by five iambic* trimeters (1457-61, 1472-6, 1486-90, 1500-4), this song introduces the heavenly omens which portend Oedipus' end. The first strophe* begins with the chorus moralising on Polyneices' fate (1447-54) and then reacting to a thunderclap (1456), while in its iambic* coda Oedipus interprets the sign according to his earlier pronouncement (94-5) as the harbinger of his death, urging someone to bring Theseus. The chorus' antistrophe* expresses their fear at another thunderclap (1462-3), while (iambic* coda) Oedipus repeats the import of the sign and his request to fetch Theseus (1472-6). The second strophe* opens with another thunderclap comment (1477-8) and is essentially a prayer for safety (1479-85), while in its coda Oedipus expresses his anxiety that Theseus should arrive in time, simply (as he tells Antigone) to receive the benefit he had earlier promised (1486-90). In the second antistrophe* the chorus urge the absent Theseus to turn up (1491-9), and he appears, to deliver its iambic* coda (*aud. right*), asking the reason for their summons (1500-4).

Fourth episode B (1505-55)

This short episode opens with Oedipus instructing Theseus in the meaning of the thunderclaps (1505-17) and then the maintenance of his cult, which is to be conducted over a tomb whose exact location is to remain a mystery, except to Theseus and his successors eternally (1518-41). Oedipus now turns guide to his children, and tells them to follow him as he moves off into the grove (1542-52) (*into the skênê*),[12] with a final blessing for Theseus and his city (1552-5).

Fourth stasimon (1556-78)

In the strophe* (1556-67) of this once again predominantly dochmiac* song (indicating perturbation), the chorus address Persephone and Hades, praying for a relatively painless death for Oedipus; in the antistrophe* (1568-78), they repeat essentially the same appeal, this time to the Eumenides, Cerberus and Death himself.

Exodos A (1579-1669)

A messenger arrives (*from the skênê*) to announce Oedipus' death to the chorus. He divulges several details about the place he reached, naming the 'brazen threshold' (1590-1), the place where many paths meet (1592), where the pledges of Theseus and Peirithous have their memorial in a 'hollow basin' (1593), near the 'Thorician stone' (1595), the 'hollow pear tree' and the 'stony tomb' (1596). Here Oedipus removes his filthy clothes and, after injunctions to his daughters, is washed and clothed afresh (1598-1605). Another thunderclap from Zeus brings forth weeping from Antigone and Ismene, and his comforting speech to them, at which more weeping (1606-23). A divine voice interrupts, calling Oedipus to his fate (1623-8), and he summons Theseus in order to entrust his daughters to the Athenian king (1629-37). His final speech directs his children to leave the place, with only Theseus to remain (1638-44). They do so but turn round to see Oedipus gone, and Theseus shielding himself as if from a divine sight, and then saluting both earth and Olympus (1645-55). A final aporetic section about the precise nature of Oedipus' death – it was 'marvellous' (1665) – concludes the report (1656-66), and a small exchange with the chorus announces the arrival of the sisters (1667-9) (*from the skênê*) before his own (unmarked) departure (*aud. right*).

Kommos (1670-1750)

Comprising two strophic* pairs (1670-96 / 1697-1723 and 1724-36 / 1737-50), the first of very mixed rhythms (including iambic*, trochaic*, dactylic* and aeolic*), and the second predominantly iambic* and trochaic*, this exchange between the sisters and the chorus laments the loss of Oedipus, expresses their intention to return to Thebes, but ends with them at a loss as to how to achieve it.

Exodos B (1751-79)

In this final (anapaestic*) scene, Theseus now appears (*from the skênê*) and briefly admonishes their lamentation (1751-3); they ask to see their father's grave, a request gently but firmly refused (1754-67), and then for his help to return to Thebes, which he grants (1768-76).[13] The chorus close the play with a final admonition that this story does not require lamentation, for everything is as it should be (1777-9), and they exit (*aud. right*).

METRICAL APPENDIX

It is important to remember the difference in delivery between episodes and *stasima*. The interplay between characters during episodes is generally delivered as *speech*, and usually in *iambic* ($\cup$ –) rhythm. The symbols here denote an alternation between a light ($\cup$) and a heavy syllable (–), the light syllable taking less time to pronounce than the heavy, and it is this alternation which gives Greek poetry its rhythm. The chorus, on the other hand, sings its *stasima*, which are constructed from a variety of rhythms, not all of which signify anything particular about its content.[14] Of course, actors could sing too, as the *amoibaia* in this play show.

Song was constructed in *strophes* (lit. 'turn', thought to indicate choral movement)[15] and *antistrophes* ('counterturn'), units of metrical patterns which responded to one another exactly, and frequently closed with an *epode* of different pattern; together these units formed a *triadic* structure. Songs without such responsion are called *astrophic*. There were a number of different rhythms, including *aeolic* or *choriambic* (– ∪ ∪ –), *anapaestic* (∪ ∪ –, frequently used by the chorus entering and leaving the *orchestra*), *dochmiac* (∪ – – ∪ –, generally used for emotionally heightened activity or description), and *trochaic* (– ∪).

3

The Oedipus Myth and the *OC*

The purpose of this chapter is not to give a detailed history of the Oedipus myth,[1] but to see how Sophocles sought to locate this particular version within that narrative continuum.

1. The landscape

Tragedy is blessed poetry beyond all, since the stories are recognised by the audience from the very start, before anyone even speaks; so the poet only needs to make a suggestion. For if I say only 'Oedipus', they know all the rest: that his father was Laius, his mother Jocasta, who his daughters were, who his sons, what this man will suffer, what he has done.

This fragment from the comic poet Antiphanes (189 KA) shows not only the popularity of the Oedipus myth in late fifth-century Athens, but also the audience's familiarity with that material.[2] Mythological narrative was a question not just of 'filling out' gaps in famous stories, but of constructing new pathways through an already crowded landscape. In doing so, Greek poets could not move in utterly new directions, for instance in saving Hector from Achilles, or leaving Troy unsacked. Innovations were still possible but, despite the open agonism with which they sometimes treated their predecessors, poets worked closely and necessarily within the established landscape: for the new to be believable, it had to accommodate itself to the old, to grant to the audience that the stories they knew were not very far from the truth.

Knowledge of that background is therefore essential if we are to attempt to place ourselves in the shoes – or on the benches – of the *OC*'s first audience. But this is no easy task. There is no single version of any myth, with local and regional variants exerting their influence on broader ('panhellenic') traditions, and with a number of different authors (in several media) seeking to exploit and recompose the stories in order to fit audience needs and expectations across the Greek world. Many of these alternatives have disappeared, leaving little or no trace; often even those traces are extremely controversial, for the records on which we depend for these early stories are the work of later authors (scholiasts, epitomators, bibliophiles) who functioned in a fundamentally antiquarian manner, combining different stories and accounts to give 'the' authoritative version.

Another problem arises when talking about the audience's knowledge, for no single audience member must have been exposed to exactly the same versions as any other. One way the playwrights coped with this was to employ allusions and flashbacks designed to delimit the scope of their own narrative, and indicate the directions they would take. Euripides was famous for doing this in his *prologoi* by having speakers come out on stage to set out the relevant information (cf. Aristophanes *Frogs* 945-50), but Sophocles was more given to having an opening conversation between two characters. Given the poets' concern to keep their audiences in the picture, as it were, it is not entirely unrealistic to try to reconstruct the range of narrative alternatives already known to that audience. As long as we recognise the gaps in our knowledge, and not push the evidence too far, the exercise should not prove dangerous.

2. The avenues open

Below is a list of the features in Oedipus' story which *might* have been known to Sophocles' audience (those preceded by an asterisk are the *OC*'s choices). The earliest known *explicit* witness to the detail is given after a dash (–), of which those marked with a crux (†) are fragmentary and witnessed only in sources later than Sophocles:

[1] rape of Chrysippus by Laius – †*Oedipodea* arg. 3-4 Bernabé
*[2] oracle warning about the birth of Oedipus given to Laius and Jocasta – Aeschylus *Seven against Thebes* 742-50
*[3] Oedipus' murder of Laius – Homer *Od.* 11.273-4
[4] Oedipus' slaying of the Sphinx – Hesiod *Th.* 326

[5] Oedipus' slaying of the Teumessian Fox – Corinna 672 *PMG*

*[6] Oedipus' incest with Jocasta (or Epicasta) – Homer *Od.* 11.272-3

*[7] Polyneices, Eteocles, Antigone and Ismene the children from Jocasta – Aeschylus *Seven against Thebes* 926ff. OR

[7a] Polyneices, Eteocles, Antigone and Ismene the children from Euryganeia – †*Oedipodea* arg. 27-9 Bernabé

*[8] Jocasta's (or Epicasta's) suicide directly after incest discovered – Homer *Od.* 11.277-9 OR

[8a] Jocasta's suicide after the death of Eteocles and Polyneices – Euripides *Phoenician Women* 1427-59

*[9] self-blinding of Oedipus – Aeschylus *Seven Against Thebes* 783-4

*[10] Oedipus' banishment and exile from Thebes – Sophocles *OT* 1436f. OR

[10a] Oedipus' continued rule, death and funeral games being celebrated there – Homer *Il.* 23.679-80; *Od.* 11.275-6

*[11] Oedipus' curse(s) on his sons while in Thebes – †*Thebaid* F 2 & 3 Bernabé[3]

*[12] conflict between Polyneices and Eteocles for control of Thebes – Hesiod *WD* 162-3; *Iliad* 4.376-98

*[13] Polyneices the elder – Aeschylus *Seven against Thebes* *passim*[4] OR

[13a] Eteocles the elder – Euripides *Phoenician Women* 71f.

*[14] hero cult in Athens – Euripides *Phoenician Women* 1703-7

Some of these details are more common than others, and Jennifer March has argued that the story undergoes radical change in the fifth century, when the children are first said to come from the incestuous marriage [7], along with exile [10] and blinding [9].[5] One could easily understand that the mostly Athenian sources might emphasise or make up more unpleasant elements, for Athens and Thebes were in constant conflict throughout this period, and their rivalry helps to explain the prominence and treatment of Theban subjects in Attic drama.[6] When Pindar stresses the fact of genealogy as a compensatory feature in Oedipus' story (*Olympian* 2.38-47) in spite of his terrible deeds (the poem's dedicatee, Theron of Acragas, claimed descent from Thersandrus, son of Polyneices through the daughter of Adrastus), he's probably following the earlier, non-Athenian tale; he may not have known of incestuous children at all. Nonetheless, March is perhaps a little too confident, as the pre-fifth-century sources are simply too exiguous for us to be certain about the story's details. We can, nonetheless, be certain that the basic outline was well set before Sophocles returned to the character in the *OC*, and (so long as we avoid dogmatism in identifying factual novelties or making too much of them) his treatment of the myth may show us how he received and recreated mythology.

Running down the list above, we see that the traditional kernel of parricide [3] and incest [6] lies at the root of the *OC*, and Sophocles follows the other Attic sources in having Antigone, Ismene, Eteocles and Polyneices mothered by Jocasta [7] (*OC* 330, 525-38), in depicting Oedipus' blindness [9] (1), and in exiling him from Theban territory [10]. Additionally, Sophocles refers to the oracle [2] received by Laius and Jocasta (969-73) and the war between Eteocles and Polyneices [12] (367-81), and also makes the latter the elder brother [13] (1293-4). A few items are inferred rather than explicitly mentioned, such as the defeat of the Sphinx [4] (539-41), which may also explain the silence about Jocasta's suicide [8],[7] though scholars continue to disagree about whether or not the story of Chrysippus' rape by Laius [1], whose consequent cursing by Pelops (Chrysippus' father) would explain the multigenerational suffering of the Labdacids, was an early part of the legend.[8]

3. New paths

A. Oracles
In developing the role of oracles in Oedipus' life [2],[9] Sophocles speaks of several delivered after Oedipus' exile from Thebes (353f.), and Ismene brings news of yet another concerning the significance of his assistance in the coming war (389f.). By taking this known quantity and multiplying it, Sophocles has caused his treatment to grow organically within the received tradition, specifically his own earlier story (*OT* 787-93), where Oedipus tells Jocasta how Apollo had revealed to him that he would kill his father and marry his mother. In the *OC*, Oedipus' reference to this 'first' oracle (87-95) expands that statement to include instructions on his final place of rest and the benefits which his tomb will confer on its land.

Euripides had already done this in his *Phoenician Women* (1403-7) of 411-409 BC, but for Sophocles the motif comes to play a vital role in the *OC*'s motivation, where the 'new' version of this first oracle connects an established event in the play's prehistory (the warning) with Oedipus' death and heroisation at its end. This expanded oracle becomes part of that prehistory when it is joined by a row of such messages delivered by Ismene to the wandering Oedipus (353-6), for it is, in effect, one in a series. The poet clinches its (appearance of) traditional authenticity by linking it with the most recent oracle (387-90), about his fate and the numinous power of his tomb, which will drive the *praxis* of the play itself. The oracular ring created is mutually supportive: every later instance summons and recreates the earliest.

B. Curses

This careful strategy can also be seen in Oedipus' curses on his sons [11]. Before the tragedians (as far as we can tell), these were delivered while Oedipus was still in Thebes, and caused either by an error in table setting (*Thebaid* F 2 Bernabé) or by providing him with an inferior portion of meat (*Thebaid* F 3 Bernabé).[10] In the *OC*, however, Oedipus repeatedly curses his sons: firstly in the presence of Antigone and Ismene (421-30) after the latter had told him of the strife which has broken out between the brothers; secondly in front of Creon (787-90) after the latter's speech persuading him to return to Thebes; thirdly on the failure of Creon's attempt to seize Oedipus, though in more general terms ('you and your whole *genos*' = 'race' / 'family' 868); fourthly to Polyneices himself (1375-82) in response to his son's entreaties to help him attack Thebes.

The sheer weight of these imprecations has impressed itself on scholars, who focused (as had ancient critics) on the apparent triviality in the curse motivations in the pre-*OC* stories,[11] concluding that Sophocles here makes them more justified: an apparently unimportant transgression gives way to ill treatment, thus (among other things) lending greater weight to the heroisation theme which runs through much of the play, and adding to our understanding of Oedipus' greatness and implacability. Certainly the restriction or reorientation of the curse to the present circumstances would make a great deal of dramatic sense in these terms.

On the other hand, several references in these passages could

3. The Oedipus Myth and the OC

be taken to refer to the 'original' curses laid on his sons in Thebes itself, thus indicating the pre-*OC* story. Lewis Campbell argued that Oedipus' reference to a prior imprecation (1375-6 'such a curse on you two (i.e. his sons) did I raise up before / and now I call them to come as my allies') should be linked with the *Thebaid* and *Oedipodea*, while Richard Jebb simply referred it back to the *OC*'s first curse (421-30).[12] However, Oedipus even in that first passage referred to the 'fated strife' between the sons (421-2), where Ismene also speaks of the 'destruction of the family of old' (369) as the factor initially discouraging the sons from claiming power in Thebes, and Polyneices himself mentions Oedipus' *Erinys* as the cause of the fraternal strife (1298-1300). If nothing else, Sophocles has given enough warrant for those so inclined to link these curses with the earlier (attested) ones.

Does an exclusive answer to this question really matter? Though Oedipus' anger might appear better motivated by restricting the reference simply to this play, the question of his justification on this issue (and others) is not at all straightforward.[13] In a very real sense, there is a basic continuity in his character between epic and tragedy, in that his harshness helps to explain his history and sufferings. Fundamentally the same quality is illuminated by these curses, with or without epic precedent.

More importantly, the ambiguity could actually be deliberate. After all, his audiences already knew of the paternal curse and its importance; in refusing to rule out those previous curses, and at the same time constructing his own in such close alignment to them, Sophocles makes his own treatment seem more believable, because it is more recognisable, better supported by precedent. As with the similarly multiplied oracle, the authority of the curses in the *OC* is established because the poet works *with* the audience's familiarities, not by ruling them out.[14] The audience will still focus on the relevance of these curses for the *OC*, whether or not they summon the epic tradition to mind. The important thing is that the curses have room to move, and significance within Sophocles' own narrative.

C. Exile and hero cult(s)
A similarly subtle and inclusive recreation of tradition can be observed in Sophocles' treatment of the story about Oedipus' exile from Thebes [10], and its connection with hero cult in

Athenian territory **[14]**. Exile was far from an automatic narrative choice, even for an Athenian author: Aeschylus has Oedipus die in Thebes (*Seven against Thebes* 914, 1004), as had Sophocles himself in the *Antigone* (899-902), while in Euripides' *Phoenician Women* he leaves Thebes of his own accord in obedience to an oracle of Apollo (1703-7; see below). Nonetheless, it was an avenue already chosen by Sophocles in the *OT*, and perhaps known to Pindar (*Pythian* 4.263-9).[15]

Obviously in the *OC* these two elements depend on one other; exile is the prerequisite for his presence in Athens and for the hostility towards Thebes which he will show as a cult hero. Indeed, although the epic tradition appears to know none of this, it seems reasonably certain that Oedipus' cult, as well as its association with Athens in general and Colonus in particular, was not invented by Sophocles; above all, the evidence of Euripides (*Phoenician Women* 1703-7) appears rather persuasive:[16]

Oed. Now the oracle, my child, of Loxias comes to its end.
Ant. Which? Will you really speak of evils in addition to these evils?
Oed. (it says) that I must wander and die in Athens.
Ant. Where? Which tower of Atthis will receive you?
Oed. Holy Colonus, the home of the horse-god (i.e. Poseidon).

Pausanias (second century AD) (1.30.4) and Valerius Maximus (first century AD) (5.3.3) knew of this cult, but the former also knew of one on the Areopagus in Athens itself (1.28.6) connected with the *Semnai Theai* ('Reverend Goddesses' – another title for the Eumenides). Androtion (fourth century BC), whose account is similar to Sophocles', also knew of Oedipus' connection with Colonus, but associated his supplication with Demeter and Athene *Polioukhos* ('city-holder').[17] Moreover, Lysimachus (second century BC) places his tomb at Eteonos in Boeotia,[18] and Thebes could have mounted a claim as well (*Il.* 23.679-80; *Od.* 11.275-6), though we do not know of any cult there.[19]

Again, it is difficult to know how old some of these stories are, and how far they depend on the *OC* itself. If alternative claims were known to his audience, then the playwright might have alluded to them, just as with the curses. The fact that Sophocles has the Thebans design to bury him under their control but not

in Theban territory itself (399-400, 406-7, 784-6) might be a
reference to the claims of Eteonos: Lysimachus says that the
Thebans were deterred from burying him in their own territory
on the grounds of his pollution (a factor to which Ismene refers
406-7), so they buried him in the territory of a village called
Keos, whose inhabitants removed the corpse in secret to Demeter's sanctuary in Eteonos.[20] Moreover, in Androtion's version
(as in Sophocles'), Oedipus asks Theseus not to tell anybody the
location of his resting place, though not for any reason associated with his cult;[21] he was instead afraid that his corpse would
be mistreated.

We may need to factor in the question of creative ambiguity
once more. Later sources knew of a cult of Oedipus' tomb on the
Areopagus in Athens in conjunction with the *Semnai Theai* and
another cult in Colonus, where Oedipus shared an *hêrôion*
('hero shrine') with Adrastus.[22] If this duplication is old enough
to have been known to Sophocles – and the passage from the
Phoenician Women is no guarantee either way, for Euripides
may not be specifying Colonus as his *burial* place – then Sophocles in the *OC* conflates two real-life cults into one. If it is not
sufficiently ancient, then the playwright is transferring a cult
to Colonus from the city centre, or vice versa, or even making
one up entirely.[23]

Note again, however, the careful inclusiveness with which
Sophocles treats these claims, for he is very imprecise about the
place of Oedipus' tomb. Everything in the play (e.g. 87-93, 411,
644-6) until the thundercrashes has suggested that Oedipus is
to be located in Colonus, yet the poet goes out of his way to avoid
saying that the tomb is definitely there. Firstly, when speaking
to Theseus, Oedipus says (1520-3):

> I will lead the way straightaway to the place,
> (I) untouched by any guide, where I must die.
> And tell this to none of men,
> neither where it is hid nor in which region it lies.

This seems to imply that even the place of his disappearance is
to be kept secret, yet the following messenger speech gives some
fairly detailed information about that location, though none of
the apparent details are certainly known to us (1590-7):[24]

And when he came to the sheer threshold,
rooted from the earth with brazen steps,
he stood on one of the many branching paths,
near the hollow basin, where the pledges
of Theseus and Peirithous lie, always faithful.
From there, standing midway between the Thorician rock
and the hollow pair tree and on the marble tomb
he took his seat; then he loosed his filthy clothes.

Here Oedipus stays until he dismisses his children and keeps
Theseus with him (1629-46). In other words, the messenger's
description seems to make clear the identity of the place 'where
I must die' (1521), which fits ill with the earlier instruction to
Theseus. Nonetheless, the secrecy enjoined in 1520-3 is still
applied to the location of the tomb, for Theseus explicitly avers
to Antigone and Ismene (1760-3):

O children, that man forbade me
that any mortal approach these places
or address
the holy tomb, which he holds.

This serves a very useful purpose, in that the actual resting
place of Oedipus is left open, but a secret nonetheless.[25] Indeed,
the injunction that its location is to be handed down only from
one ruler to the next (1518-34) builds some flexibility into the
narrative, and allows room for cultic development between the
time of Theseus and Sophocles.[26] In fact the play may even be
said to motivate such a development – for the original reception
in Colonus provides sufficient reason for its contemporary cult,
while the physical description of the tomb at the play's end
recalls suggestively the physical features of the 'other' contemporary cult of Oedipus on the Areopagus, especially the 'sheer
threshold' (*katarraktên odon OC* 1590; cf. also 56-7), the presence of a temple to Demeter *Eukhlous* ('of the good shoot' 1600),
and the association with the Eumenides.[27] The playwright, in
other words, manages to leave room for something of both cults
or traditions. Each is supported, each is justified – neither is
excluded.[28]

Nonetheless, given the fact that most of the sources postdate
Sophocles, the question of 'novelty' is a very hard one to answer,
and perhaps also the wrong one to ask. Whether the cult in

3. The Oedipus Myth and the OC

Colonus was known to Sophocles' audience in the form he depicts it, the *OC* does something 'new' in a tragic context by placing the question of hero cult at its very centre, to an extent definitely not countenanced by Euripides, for whom it is little more than a passing reference, another example of his typical closure with the establishment of a cult.[29] By contrast, Sophocles takes something already known to his audience in a variety of forms, and transforms it by giving it greater emphasis, by making it a central theme. This novelty is supported by his earlier one, with regard to the original oracle: that 'new' first oracle guarantees the cult, and the cult becomes the manifestation of the power inherent in Apollo's initial guidance.

In discussing Sophocles' treatment of these themes, we have observed his careful recreation of elements already known to the audience, and the subtlety with which their knowledge is invoked and manipulated. Startling changes in those elements and their ordering are avoided, and the playwright works by reorienting the story rather than renovating it wholesale, bringing as many of his audience with him as he can, with new emphases and intimations rather than new facts.

4. Previous journeys

Several of the *OC*'s mythical directions owed a great deal to Sophocles' *Oedipus Tyrannus*,[30] and it has been an ancient and modern truism that the *OC* is a conclusion to the *OT*.[31] In common with that play (date uncertain),[32] Sophocles used once more the exile motif, and seemed to refer explicitly to the *OT*'s rather troubled ending, where the exile of Oedipus is apparently put into doubt by Creon's decision to send another messenger to Delphi to enquire what they should do now (*OT* 1438ff.). Oedipus in the *OC* may well be referring to this particular scene, specifically the hesitancy over the timing and motivation for his banishment, when he twice tells his version of these events. The first comes when he reacts angrily to the news of the oracle about his benefit to Thebes, as he abuses his absent sons for failing to prevent his exile (431-44); he claims that his initial desire was to be stoned to death (433-5), but that later on (when he had become convinced he'd been too harsh on himself!) he was then exiled (437-41). The second falls during his furious denunciation of Creon (765-71), in which he claims that Creon had frustrated his initial desire to be exiled, only to fulfil it when Oedipus had decided he no longer wished it.

As we shall argue in Chapter 4, these two narratives are in fact mutually exclusive, but they help to bridge the gap with the earlier story. Admittedly, there is no mention of Apollo's instructions to exile Laius' murderer but, when Ismene explains the reluctance of the Thebans to receive Oedipus back into their territory because of his pollution (407), it is a necessary inference that his expulsion must have had something to do with that fact. Though other narrative courses are possible in the revelation of the murder and the subsequent *miasma*,[33] pollution and its consequences were natural objects of divine attention. The *OC*'s silence on this point cannot rule out either the original oracle from the *OT* or the subsequent confirmation of that instruction, which is all that Creon seeks at the end of the earlier play.[34] These two narratives therefore fit well with the circumstances prevailing at the *OT*'s end – his initial, apparently frustrated, desire to die / be exiled is now replaced by the city's command of banishment. Together, the stories serve two interrelated purposes; they explain the progression from the *OT*'s eager exile restrained by Creon to the *OC*'s angry exile sought by Creon, and they do so while emphasising the continuity in Oedipus' anger between the two plays, while adding resentment and illogicality to the mixture.[35]

But the relationship between the *OT* and *OC* goes well beyond narrative bridging. Indeed, Bernd Seidensticker (above all) has traced a constant intertextual relationship on several levels. The most obvious is the general progression in Oedipus' fortunes from dishonour to honour, reversing the *OT*'s pattern:

OT			*OC*
Oedipus as mighty hero	A	E	Oedipus the blind beggar
Oedipus and Teiresias	B	D	Oedipus' 'interrogation'
Oedipus and Creon	C	C	Oedipus and Creon
Oedipus' 'interrogation'[36]	D	B	Oedipus and Polyneices
Oedipus the blind beggar	E	A	Oedipus as mighty hero

This is not a complete map of either play, with figures as important as Jocasta, Theseus and Antigone left out of account, but it captures the basic relationship between them. An aesthetic of reversal dominates here, structuring the poet's repetition of themes and roles, and in many forms. For instance, Oedipus is reduced from the mighty figure whose guidance is sought at the start of the *OT* to a helpless figure guided into the palace (and eventually out of the city) by Creon; so he begins the *OC* guided by his daughter and ends it by guiding his daughters and Theseus to the location of his death. Furthemore, the poet repeats the *OT*'s theme of sight and blindness, but again by turning it around; whereas Oedipus' sight (intellect) was shown wanting in the *OT* and taken away from him at the end of the play, in the *OC* he regains sight of a sort in being able to see the end of his sufferings.[37]

Aside from thematic progressions, individual scenes are mirrored, and a creative mixture of reversal and continuity controls the parallelism. To begin with, the *prologoi* are structured in exactly the same way (A = E in the scheme above): Oedipus is the first speaker, his initial speech (13 verses) is split between an introductory description of the situation (8 verses), and then an address to the interlocutor beginning at verse 9 with *alla* ('but').[38] An 'initiating' figure arrives (Creon *OT*; the Athenian stranger *OC*) who does not wish to speak unless the location of the intercourse is altered (inside the palace *OT*; out of the Eumenides' grove *OC*), an objection Oedipus overrides, at least partially in the process of bestowing a benefit to the locality (protection of Thebes *OT*; hinted gain to Athens *OC*). Oracles are similarly important in each of the *prologoi*, driving the action of the entire play: Creon's delivery of Apollo's instructions in the *OT* will eventually place Oedipus into a dishonour only reversed by Oedipus' remembrance of his own oracle in the *OC*.

A similar series of mirrorings may be traced in the *exodoi* of the two plays (E = A). First, Oedipus entrusts his daughters to an authority figure (Creon *OT* 1459f.; Theseus *OC* 1631f.), who accompanies him off stage into the *skênê* (before the departure *OT*; after it *OC*),[39] though of course the Creon-led Oedipus of the *OT* is now leading Theseus in the *OC*. Thematically, an appeal by Oedipus to the power of light (*OT* 1183; *OC* 1549-50) precedes his departure, and is followed in the *OT* by Oedipus' blinding, in the *OC* by his manifestation of an 'inner sight'. After the departure, a messenger speech details the evolution in Oedipus' sight: in the *OT* a 'deity', rather than any of his colleagues (*OT* 1258-9), leads Oedipus to blind himself; in the

OC Oedipus and a 'god' (*OC* 1626-30), rather than any of his colleagues (*OC* 1588-9), lead Theseus and the others to the proper place. The earlier staining of his clothes and face with blood (*OT* 1268-79) is reversed when he removes his clothes, is washed and dressed anew (*OC* 1597-1603). Each of these messenger speeches is followed by a *kommos* – between the chorus and Oedipus in the *OT*, and his daughters in the *OC* – in which everybody wishes for death and bewails the circumstance (*OT* 1297-1367; *OC* 1670-1750), and after which a ruler arrives to direct the subsequent fate of the characters (Creon *OT*; Theseus *OC*).

While we find simple correspondences of this sort, where elements in the same stage of each play mirror one another, we also find chiastic relationships. For instance, the *exodos* of the *OT* and the *prologos* of the *OC* show significant parallels (E = E in the diagram above): an apparently helpless, blind old figure nevertheless dominates the scene, notwithstanding the efforts of others to control him. This is no surprise, for the opening scene of the *OC* enacts what is expected at the end of the *OT*, but chiasmus is pursued quite persistently throughout the *OC*. The confrontation between Polyneices and Oedipus in the *OC* (1254-1446) reflects powerfully that between Oedipus and Teiresias in the *OT* (300-462) (B = B): in both scenes a deter-mined young man faces an older blind figure supported by a youth (*OT* young boy; *OC* Antigone) possessed of extraordinary knowledge, who is initially silent in the face of the younger man's request for assistance, but then becomes bitter in his refusal. Indeed, both Teiresias and Oedipus end their speeches with furious denunciations, and a negative prediction about the future, of their interlocutors (*OT* 417-25, 452-62; *OC* 1370-96). The parallels between the situations of the *OT*'s Oedipus and the *OC*'s Polyneices are made clear when Oedipus labels his son his 'murderer' (*OC* 1361), just as Teiresias in the *OT* had openly stated that Oedipus was the killer of Laius, and at the same time the 'murderer' (*OT* 460) of his own father.

Similarly, the conflict between Oedipus and Creon in the *OC* (720-1043) shows considerable parallels with its mirror scene in the *OT* (513-677), the 'first' conflict between the same charac-ters (C = C). In both scenes, a character with greater official authority (Oedipus *OT*; Creon *OC*) faces one of less authority (Creon *OT*; Oedipus *OT*) who is assisted at a crucial moment of impending violence by the arrival of a third person (Jocasta *OT*;

48

Theseus *OC*) to prevent that violence. In both scenes, Creon begins by addressing the internal audience before he is rebuked for his brazenness by Oedipus (*OT* 512-31, 532-5; *OC* 728-39, 761-4). So the mirroring works, once again, both by drawing similarities and emphasising the reversals in situation. One of the latter, of course, is that Oedipus' anger is at least a little more justified against Creon in the *OC*, who is being duplicitous here as he was not in the *OT*.[40] The last of these mirror scenes are the 'interrogations' (D = D), where Oedipus engages in *amoibaion* with the chorus about his identity. In the *OT* this occurs after the blinding (1297-1368), in the *OC* during the *parodos* as the chorus search the area around the grove for the trespasser (138-254); the link is established at the outset of each scene by the chorus' shared statements of horror about Oedipus in explicitly visual terminology (*OT* 1297-1307; *OC* 140-1).

Obviously, the *OC* is not merely or only a reversed image of the *OT*. For instance, while Jocasta in the *OT* and Antigone in the *OC* have similar functions – female relatives (which in this family always means more than usual) attempting to soothe Oedipus' anger directed at a kinsman (Creon *OT*; Polyneices *OC*) – they do so in stages of their plays other than those which the map above might lead us to expect (C = B). Furthermore, Jocasta also mirrors the function of Theseus (C = C) in arriving just in time to prevent violence between Oedipus and Creon, as we saw. Nonetheless, the constant engagement with the structures and roles of the *OT* largely justify Seidensticker's description of the relationship as 'new people in the old roles'.[41] The significance of this observation should not be overplayed, for Sophocles almost certainly didn't intend the *OC* to be performed together with the *OT*. Therefore, the interpretations of the drama in the following chapters will proceed primarily from the *OC* itself, and adduce intertextual relationships only in order to supplement conclusions already reached.

Sophocles did not treat the Oedipus myth only in the *OT*, and cases have been made for the *OC*'s intertextual engagement with a number of other plays, notably Sophocles' own *Antigone* (undated),[42] and the *Phoenician Women* of Euripides (411-409 BC).[43] Certainly the final scene of the *OC*, in which Antigone and Ismene bewail the fate of their father and then express a determination to return to Thebes[44] to prevent fraternal slaughter, when coupled with the earlier emphasis which Polyneices had laid on the need for his family to take thought for his burial should he fail in his aims (1405-13), would make a ready connection between the narrative material of the former play.[45] More precisely perhaps, the small contest between Antigone and Ismene (1724-36), in which the former demands to be shown the grave of her father while the latter cautions against it because it is not 'right' / 'lawful' (*themis*) for them to see the tomb, displays in a nutshell the conflict of the former's wilful determination (again about mourning and burial) and the latter's hesitance to act against authority which is central to their interactions in the *Antigone*.[46] Other possible hints may include Oedipus' curse on Creon in his old age (868-70), which is largely fulfilled in the course of the *Antigone*, and Polyneices' reference to Antigone's future reputation for caring for her brother's corpse (1411-13), while the constant statements of affection between Antigone and Polyneices (1415, 1439-43) would fit well with her somewhat one-sided concern for him in the *Antigone*.[47]

Finally, Euripides' *Phoenician Women*. Aside from the fact that 'the *tableau vivant* that opens *Oedipus Coloneus* recalls the one that closes *Phoenissae*',[48] Mueller-Goldingen argues that Sophocles derived from that source the role of Antigone as her father's guide; the idea that Oedipus was still alive when civil war broke out between the brothers; the presence, self-defence and relatively positive characterisation of Polyneices;[49] while the role of Antigone, who tries to deflect the terrible future of her family, may well recollect also the similar attempts of Jocasta in Euripides' play.

Of course, one is entitled to ask whether detailed engagement of this sort is possible. After all, texts of these plays were not widely available, and there were well over a thousand pieces – tragedies, satyr-plays, comedies – performed at the dramatic festivals in Athens during the fifth century. Would the audience have been thinking of Sophocles' previous versions any more than any of the countless versions by many other performers, authors or painters, for that matter? No definitive answer to this question is possible, and the links suggested with the *Antigone* and *Phoenician Women* are neither so pervasive nor important as to render such an answer necessary. But the *OT–OC* nexus is something different, and the relationship between the plays is so thorough and varied that it would be reductive to deny it.

3. The Oedipus Myth and the OC

We can conclude the final section of this chapter very swiftly. Sophocles' *OC* engaged not only with 'the myth' of Oedipus but also with its popular and important *tragic* treatments. One is struck by the depth and immediacy of that engagement, which tells us something about the nature of the tragic competitions, the authors who participated at them, and the audiences who experienced them. Though the landscape may have been crowded, the paths through it were for that reason all the more interesting.

4

Oedipal Accounts

Oedipus' attitude to guilt and responsibility defines his character. He is as passionate in his own defence as he is convinced of others' guilt, and his presentation has been so persuasive that scholars often term him 'objectively' guilty of his famous crimes, but 'subjectively' innocent because had no knowledge of what he was doing.[1]

We begin by considering some Athenian legal norms of the fifth and fourth centuries BC, specifically the fact that intent was an important element in homicide cases.[2] The major ancient text is a reinscription of Dracon's original homicide law from the seventh century BC, dated 409/8 BC – an intriguing coincidence with the *OC*'s date – which distinguished between intentional (*hekôn*) and unintentional (*âkôn*) homicide, which were even tried in different courts (Areopagus and Palladion). Though their definition is uncertain, they were not akin to modern categories of murder and manslaughter: *hekôn* homicide included cases where intended harm led to death. Leaving aside the pollution (*miasma*) arising from killing,[3] those convicted of *hekôn* homicide suffered death and property confiscation, while *akôn* homicides were exiled until pardoned by the dead man's relatives.

Oedipus adds to this mix the two enormous taboos of parricide and incest. The former was obviously an horrendous crime, but treated legally just like other cases of homicide,[4] while incest naturally incurred tremendous opprobrium but no separate legal sanction.[5] Of course, contemporary legal norms are only indirectly useful, for the world of heroes is not the world of the audience: Oedipus is not pleading before an Athenian court. But he constantly deploys terms and concepts familiar from that context, as we shall see.

4. Oedipal Accounts

1. Oedipus on himself

The issue of Oedipus' (understanding of his) responsibility turns primarily on his three apologies (258-91, 510-48, 960-1013), their basic principle the idea that he acted in ignorance. This requires some qualification from the start, for he had been told that he was fated to kill his father and marry his mother. Though Apollo's message is never outlined (Oedipus refers glancingly to (87) 'these many evils'), its import seems to be much the same as in the *OT* (789-93), so he was not unaware that these activities were fraught with more than the usual danger.[6] But his consistent emphasis is that he did not know who Laius was when he killed him, nor Jocasta when he married her. This argument, however, is constructed so as to prevent us – or an Athenian audience – from being totally persuaded.

A. First apology (258-74)
Delivered to the chorus in order to persuade them to let him stay, his first defence speech begins by invoking Athens' reputation for mercy (258-62), before relating it to his own case (263-74):

> And where is this (sc. reputation) in my case, if you raise me
> from these seats and then drive me out,
> fearing my name alone? For it is not my body
> nor my deeds you fear; since you must know that my
> deeds were more suffered than done,
> if I must speak to you of my maternal and paternal affairs,
> for which you fear me; this I know
> very well. And yet how am I base by nature,
> when I paid back what I had suffered, so that if I had acted
> with full knowledge, not even so would I have been base?
> But now, knowing nothing, I came where I came,
> and my destruction was attempted knowingly by those at whose
>   hands I suffered.

First, the claim that he is not 'base by nature' seems to sit ill with the history of Laius' house. Something was indeed wrong 'by nature' (*physei*), for *physis* refers to the totality of family inheritance. Though Sophocles does not explicitly mention Laius' cursing or wrongdoings, no audience member could have been unaware of the family's troubled history.[7] Secondly,

53

Oedipus' claim of passivity (267) also seems somewhat question-able, not least because he then says that his actions were in some way called for, that he 'paid back' (*antedrôn*) what he had suffered from his parents (271). One cannot really have it both ways.

Thirdly, to what parental offence is he referring in 271-4, and to what action of revenge? His subsequent assertion, that he still 'would not have been base' had he known then what he was doing (271-2), must refer to his killing of Laius on the road, though this could only work legally if Laius and his men attempted to kill him (991-6). This would make it a matter of self-defence (for which Oedipus would have been acquitted in an Athenian court),[8] but he only makes this argument in his third apology, and we are not entitled to infer it here. Indeed, considering the intertext with the *OT*'s version (800-13),[9] where Oedipus freely admits that he overreacted to the actions of Laius and his men, there are serious problems with his reasoning.

In any case, the reciprocity argument could not excuse the sexual relationship with his mother (and in his second and third apologies he will claim that he was forced to marry her). But it is clear that Oedipus *is* thinking of both his parents in this passage; its introduction heralds his 'maternal and paternal affairs' (268) and, immediately after the argument in 271-2, he contrasts his own ignorance with the knowledge and intent of those who tried to kill him (i.e. when he was a baby: 273-4). All this sits ill with the important fact that he did not know of their 'offences' when he killed Laius and slept with his mother. Something else led him to do those things, and the revenge principle is both unnecessary and entirely misdirected. Notably, he makes no mention here of the oracle given to Jocasta and Laius (though he knows about it 969-73), focusing entirely on their responsibility. Indeed, he only invokes the divine in his own defence (e.g. 964-5, 998).

His somewhat muddied and partial stream of thought is caused mostly by the fact that he combines ignorance with revenge. Had Sophocles wished to make a straightforward case in Oedipus' favour, he could simply have used the former. But Sophocles does not choose this route, instead framing his history with the typical heroic principle of requiting harm.[10] This argument undermines the clarity of his case, and the passage as a whole suggests temper and resentment more than anything else.

B. Second apology (510-48)

The second apology comes in an exchange between Oedipus and the chorus, when the rather prurient old men question him about his deeds. They focus precisely on some of the messy details – incest, fathering of children / siblings – neglected in the first apology, and he is forced to talk about things he'd rather not (as later (985-6) with Creon). He consistently deploys the ignorance criterion, this time untainted by anger, and also without the need to persuade the chorus of anything, for they have already agreed to defer the issue of his supplication to their rulers (294-5). Yet once more there are problems with Oedipus' narrative, though it is difficult to analyse his arguments in detail, because textual uncertainties make a tremendous difference to the point being made.[11]

Despite that, three things are clear. First, his reluctance to speak about his history, as well as the horror it generates, suggest that his arguments do not persuade anyone that he is without taint (as again later (1132-6) when he shrinks from touching Theseus).[12] Secondly, his claim that 'in *nomos* I am pure; unknowing I came to this' (548), no matter what the textual difficulties with the previous verse, is very problematic. *Nomos* can mean both enacted legislation and general custom, though here it seems to gravitate more towards the former notion. Oedipus has not yet explicitly invoked self-defence, which would render him legally 'pure' (though the question of knowledge would be irrelevant in such a case, and so Oedipus' link between legal purity and ignorance is misplaced).[13] Nonetheless, given what the audience have been told until now (and perhaps influenced once more by the *OT* intertext), this claim is factually very dubious: his lack of knowledge about his victim's identity does not make it any the less a homicide, for which he would be arraigned in an Athenian court and sentenced (at least) to exile, and from which pollution would arise.[14]

Thirdly, this is the first time he exculpates himself explicitly of incest, and in doing so he focuses entirely on the city's role (525-6, 539-41):

> with an ill wedlock, *the city* bound me, knowing nothing,[15]
> to the doom arising from my marriage.

Ch. You suffered. **Oed.** I suffered things terrible to bear.
Ch. You acted .... **Oed.** I did not act. **Ch.** What?
Oed. *I received* a gift, which I, wretched hearted, should never
  have taken for my benefits.

Yet was Oedipus without choice? He did not have to accept the
throne of Thebes and Jocasta's hand, for power could have
passed to Creon without dynastic difficulty. Note that Oedipus
has already abused his sons for their political ambition (418-19,
425f.; see below), once more rebuking others for a failing he
shares. Further, Oedipus did know at the time that he was fated
to marry his mother, while the city had no access to this
knowledge, so his reasoning here is more emotional than logical.[16] Again, a simple declaration of ignorance would have suf-
ficed, but Sophocles is not interested in simple declarations.

C. Third apology (960-1013)

His most detailed apology is the third and final one, directed
abusively at Creon's attempt (939-59) to mollify Theseus' en-
raged reaction to the abduction of Ismene and Antigone (897-
936).[17] Creon's speech had sought to persuade Theseus that he
acted not out of contempt for Athens or its ruler, but because he
never thought the Areopagus court could want to shelter someone so stained as Oedipus; nonetheless, he only acted out of
anger because of the abuse showered on him by his kinsman.
This last element in Creon's self-exculpation ('having suffered
(*peponthôs*) these things I thought it right to pay them back
(*antidrân*)' 953) recalls Oedipus' own statement in his first
apology 'when I paid back (*antedrôn*) what I had suffered
(*pathôn*)' 271), pointing to their basic similarity.

Returning to the specific charges, Oedipus takes Creon's
points in reverse order (960-99), using a ring structure, in which
the theme of the divine frames the two precise charges:

   1. Gods (964-5)
      2. Parricide (969-77)
         3. Incest (978-88)
      2. Parricide (989-96)
   1. Gods (997-9)

The first thing to note is that, when covering the parricide, he uses the argument for self-defence in the second of the two passages (989-96), *not* the first. In that earlier passage (969-77), Oedipus is once more invoking the ignorance criterion, and again his assertion that he 'knew nothing of what he was doing' is weak – he knew that he was killing someone, certainly, enough to make the circumstance amount to homicide. When Oedipus returns to the parricide (989), his position is now changed, for he deploys the argument of self-defence for the first and only time in the play. It happens in a curiously roundabout manner (992-6), as Oedipus asks a hypothetical question of Creon as to what he would have done in the circumstance, and then further obscures its relationship with his own case by saying 'I entered upon such evils' (*toiauta* 997). This is, I repeat, the play's *only* description of Laius' death, the *only* explicit statement that Oedipus acted in self-defence. As this is a cornerstone of modern defences of his behaviour, and as it was definitely *not* part of the story in the *OT*,[18] it is remarkable that Sophocles should slip in Oedipus' strongest legal defence in such an indirect form and so late in the play. Had the playwright simply wished to acquit Oedipus, surely he would have deployed this argument much earlier. Again, Sophocles is not interested in simple judgements.

Other consequences follow. The most important is that, legally, it renders irrelevant the entirety of his previous defence – and in the first 'parricide' section of this very speech. An argument of self-defence was a sufficient answer in an Athenian court to a charge of homicide, but the ignorance criterion on which Oedipus has hitherto depended had nothing to do with such a circumstance.[19] Had Oedipus killed Laius in self-defence, even if he had known who he was, he would not have been liable for punishment in a contemporary court (as long as he could show that his assailant had struck first), though there would still be pollution attendant on parricide.[20]

Of course, legal norms should not be mapped so tightly onto the world of the play, but (aside from the fact that scholars routinely do this) Oedipus uses the legal term 'unwilling' (*âkôn*) *four* times in this speech – to describe his general situation (964) and the parricide (977), as well as the incest (987) and his narrative of it (987). The term has been used before, by the chorus to assure Oedipus that he will not be removed from his seat 'unwillingly' (177), by Antigone to describe Oedipus' actions when she's speaking with the chorus (240), and by Oedipus himself when he berates Creon for thinking that those who are 'unwilling' can be *philoi* (775). But in this speech, he only does so *before* making the argument of self-defence, as though Sophocles is pointing out structurally the exclusion zones of *âkôn* homicide and self-defence. This point is also made by the several poor uses to which Oedipus puts the 'unwilling' argument: first he describes his misfortunes in this way (964), 'for thus was it dear to the gods', but divine participation never removes mortal contribution to that process, certainly not in Oedipus' own eyes when he refused to acknowledge such a factor in his parents' case during his first apology. Secondly, when he describes the killing (977) as an 'unwilling' matter (i.e. before contending self-defence), '(since I knew) nothing of what I was doing nor those against whom I was doing it' (976), his claim is (as we have seen) specious: with or without ignorance, it is still homicide.[21]

But his difficulties with the term *akôn* become clearer when he applies it to incest (985-7): he begins by contrasting Creon's 'willing' (*hekont'* 985) mention of the matter with his own 'unwilling' marriage (*âkôn* 987), and the fact that he is 'unwilling' even to speak of it (*âkôn* 987). While the ordinary meaning of the word and its antonym is appropriate to their contrasted attitudes in speaking about it, *âkôn* is less suitable to describe the marriage itself, and highlighted by its position between two examples of its usual meaning. One could refer to Oedipus' second apology, where he said that the city 'bound' him to 'doom' and an 'evil bed', and that he was simply receiving a 'gift'. In that sense, he would be simply picking up on a previous (unpersuasive) depiction of the marriage as a matter of compulsion. But just as one could reflect on the accuracy of that earlier description, so Oedipus' rhetorical flourish should not conceal his sleight of hand with this rather important word. In sum, Sophocles festoons this speech with contemporary legal terms and norms to show his audience Oedipus confusing and conflating different circumstances and arguments, producing a case more emotionally satisfying than logically or legally rigorous.[22]

How does Oedipus come out of this? Plenty of readers have noticed the power of his rhetoric, in itself a testament to the strength and determination with which Sophocles has imbued his character. Yet the logic in his apologies is dubious. He confuses or introduces unnecessary arguments which stand in the way of what could be a very simple defence, contradicts himself within and between speeches, uses criteria in questionable ways, claims arguments for himself which he refuses to apply to others, and uses his strongest argument late and poorly.[23] As the play progresses, Sophocles increasingly manipulates legal categories and language to show Oedipus' growing sense of self-justification and belief, but at the expense of a consistent and persuasive case. To repeat, an Athenian audience is not meant to think that Oedipus should be subject to the same range of penalties as a contemporary defendant, but to reflect rather that his actions and character do not allow him to make a good case of his situation. Sophocles has him frame his defence in order that the audience see the extremity of his character and circumstance specifically in that context, and to realise how inadequately their own norms can fit such a person. To the question asked at the end of the *OT* – how does one solve a problem like Oedipus? – the *OC* answers: 'not in the lawcourts'.

2. Oedipus on others

The other pillar to Oedipus' sense of rectitude is his attitude to others, and specifically whether or not he is right to blame the Thebans, Creon and his sons for his situation. The answer depends, at least partially, on the rightness and circumstances of that exile. For Oedipus, it is a matter solely of malice (city 440-1; 'my own seed' 599-601; Creon 768-71; Polyneices 1354-7), yet there are several hints that his may not be a balanced perspective. First, Ismene refers to the fact that Oedipus' return to, and burial in, Theban territory is impossible: 'but the kindred blood does not permit that' (407).[24] Despite his initial claim to the chorus that he comes 'holy and pious' (287), Oedipus acknowledges his pollution, twice, to Theseus (600-1; 1130-6):

And it is not possible
for me ever to return, as a parricide.

And give me your right hand, my lord,
so I may touch it and kiss your head, if it is allowed.
And yet what am I saying? How could I, wretch I am,
wish to touch a man for whom there is no

indwelling stain of evil; I could not,
nor would I allow it. For only those mortals
who have experienced them can share the suffering.

Miasma, then, has some bearing on the issue (even in Oedipus' own mind), for it precludes his return and so must have had something to do with his exile. Its effect in the *OT* was the plague which beset Thebes and, to follow this intertext further,[25] we might infer that the situation at the *OT*'s end – where Creon sent for another oracle – was fulfilled before the beginning of this play, and so that exile and oracle were not unconnected. This certainly fits Oedipus' two versions of these events (431-44, 765-71), where his initial desire to die and / or be exiled from the city was not granted at the time, but forced on him later.

Yet neither Oedipus nor anybody else in the *OC* mentions any oracle in connection with the exile. However, Ismene mentions several oracles during the time when Oedipus was being banished (353-6):

And you, my child, you came to your father beforehand
bringing *all the oracles*, in secret from the Thebans,
the ones which were delivered about me, and you stood up
as my faithful guard, when *I was being driven out* of the land.

The imperfect tense of the verb in the last clause (italicised), together with the phrase 'all the oracles' (354), suggests a *process* of consultation, and one which did not begin only after his departure. If nothing else, the Thebans were receiving continuous guidance, so divine sanction could not have been unconnected with the fact of exile. Moreover, at the play's start Oedipus mentions that Apollo had told him of his exile and at least intimated the place and timing of his death (87-95): for eventual honouring, banishment is necessary. This does not render any of the three objects of Oedipus' hate innocent. But it does mean, at the very least, that his attitude to the situation is extremely partial. That he is so elsewhere, on precisely this issue, may be seen from his penchant for invoking the gods to mitigate only his own actions (964-5).[26] However understandable it may be, Sophocles has left Oedipus using another defence he refuses to grant to others.

On the other hand, why do neither Creon nor Polyneices defend themselves with divine sanction? First, Sophocles always has Oedipus speak second, and neither Creon nor Polyneices are ever given a chance to reply to his arguments. Secondly, their purposes and circumstances give them good reason not to use the argument. For instance, Creon's first (deceptive) proposal to Oedipus pretends that the summons back to Thebes are a heartfelt call from kith and kin. He does not mention any old oracle because he doesn't want to mention the new one – the real reason for his current attempt – and this would naturally bring up the issue of the pollution involved in Oedipus' return. As already learned from Ismene (407), the Thebans cannot let him into their territory for precisely this reason, so Creon avoids mentioning the divine altogether. Oedipus' angry reply (761-99, esp. 770-1) does claim that Creon was personally responsible for his exile – with no mention of gods (obviously, for they would confound his case) – but Creon has no chance for a detailed response, as their encounter swiftly descends into abuse and violence.

Their second exchange is delivered in Theseus' presence, to whose charge of dishonouring Athens and himself Creon directs himself. He is still being deceptive, trying to claim that Oedipus' anger led him to snatch the girls and even the old man himself (though Ismene had already been seized), but the exile's rightness is simply assumed, as Creon details the crimes rendering unlikely Oedipus' reception anywhere. Though Oedipus replies with his argument of personal unwillingness and divine responsibility (above), Creon again has no opportunity to answer, for Theseus simply takes over and forces compliance with his commands.

In contrast to Creon, Polyneices freely admits his error in letting Oedipus' condition deteriorate, but nowhere attempts to excuse the fact of exile, presumably because he felt no need to do so. It is only because of the new oracle (openly mentioned 1331-2) that he feels himself free to return his father to honour in Thebes, presumably believing (unlike the Thebans) that this oracle cancels the old one, and envisages Oedipus' return. He may be wrong, because his father both will not and cannot come back, but Polyneices' error shows only his conviction. When Oedipus then claims that Polyneices *personally* caused the exile, his son has no chance to respond because he has already put a reasonable case. To argue with Oedipus in such a mood, or indeed at all, is impossible.

This has implications for his first outburst against his sons (421-60), reacting to Ismene's news of their strife (428-9; 443-4; 448-9):

> when thus dishonoured I was pushed from my fatherland
> they did not hold me nor protect me ...
>
> ... but for the sake of a *small word*,[27]
> I began my eternal wandering, an exile, a beggar, outside
>
> they have preferred, over their father, *thrones*
> *and wielding sceptres*[28] and to be ruler over the land

His complaint against them is not just that they haven't supported him in exile (428-9), but also that they did not prevent it. The former charge is undoubtedly true and admitted by Polyneices (1265-6), but the latter is much less certain. Creon was in control in Thebes at the time (something which Oedipus seems to forget later on; see below), and the sons' ability to prevent the exile was surely limited by the import of these several oracles governing Oedipus' fate. There is, however, a further item of interest here, in his initial complaint against his sons, on being told of the new oracle by Ismene (418-19):

> and then these most wicked men, hearing this (sc. the oracle),
> have set the tyranny over their desire for me?

The idea of preferring power to their father (cf. 448 above) is very significant. Unless Oedipus is rebuking his sons for not doing hitherto what Polyneices will soon try to do – i.e. approach him – he must mean that they did not persuade the Thebans, in the light of Apollo's recent statement, to call him back and restore him to the throne. They wanted it for themselves.[29]

His point is made with some prominent repeated phraseology, the 'sceptres and thrones' (*skêptra kai thronoi*) theme, deployed by Oedipus alone: to Ismene he prays that he 'who currently holds the thrones and sceptres' (425) should not remain in power, and he excoriates his sons because 'they have preferred, over their father, thrones and wielding sceptres and to be ruler over the land (448-9). When cursing Polyneices in person, he places the agency behind his exile (as he sees it) firmly at Polyneices' feet 'when you held the sceptres and thrones' (1354). The repetition of this expression in the later scene does not just point out the importance of the theme, or his sons' hypocrisy and poor record.[30] Instead, the reminiscence reminds the audience that his grievance was his sons' failure to restore him to power. The only 'sceptre' now left to Oedipus is Antigone and Ismene, as both he (1109) and Creon (848) point out.

This theme, and its repetition, shows that Oedipus is still angry at being deprived of *power* (and the chance of its restoration), and not just that his sons are ambitious. Ambition, of course, had at least something to do with Oedipus' own career, though it remains quite absent from his narratives.[31] As in his first apology, Oedipus begins from a reasonable position – a lack of support – but his anger extends the charge in several, much less justifiable (but much more interesting) directions.

Unsurprisingly, the details in Oedipus' blame narratives are also problematic. First, the superficially similar stories of his exile told to his daughters and the chorus (431-40f.) and to Creon (765-70f.) after his opening (deceptive) speech are in fact irreconcilable; in the first passage, Oedipus denies that he ever wanted exile (esp. 433), while in the second he claims he did (765-7). The discrepancy is contextually driven: in the former passage, he's excoriating his sons for not preventing his banishment, so it suits his purpose (or belief) to portray exile as entirely abhorrent. In the latter passage he's addressing the very man he accuses of the decision, contending now that his problem was with its timing. The situations are analogous, in that Oedipus contrasts his immediate desires with what was later forced on him, but their narratives are actually mutually exclusive.

Secondly, his reconstructions don't fit. When speaking to the chorus, Oedipus frames the exile as the 'city' driving him out (440-1); when speaking to Theseus he attributes the action to 'my own seed' (599-601); when abusing Creon, he blames Creon ('you pushed and cast me out' 770); finally, when speaking to Polyneices, his son is the agent ('you yourself drove out this man, your own father, / and you made him without a city and forced him to bear these robes' 1356-7). One could reconcile the first and third instances, for it is conventional in Greek heroic thought that a city is responsible for the actions of its ruler. The second might simply be considered a little exaggeration (as elsewhere). But the fourth passage cannot be reconciled: Ismene made it clear that the brothers' strife for power was recent, before which Creon had ruled. At any rate, he was certainly the ruler in the narrative contained within Oedipus' abuse in the second passage. Indeed, Ismene does not make it clear that Polyneices ever held sway in Thebes, and Polyneices' own version of these events is similarly indirect. So, who is to blame, or should we rather conclude that Oedipus is not a particularly reliable source of information?[32]

Context and rhetoric influence the way he frames the responsibility of the three groups. To the chorus, i.e. a group, he blames the Theban polity as a whole. This convinces them of his hostility to the Theban community, and so his desire to benefit Athens as a community ('I come holy and pious and bearing / benefit *to these citizens*' 287-8).[33] When explaining to a sceptical Theseus why he won't return to Thebes, Oedipus focuses on his sons both because maltreatment by *sons* is particularly galling, and also because it remains an issue within the monarch's immediate family, which is always rather important for tragic autocrats. When discrediting Creon in front of Theseus, he blames Creon; when abusing Polyneices, he blames him. While the first and third passages show his ability to shape his story for his audience, his alterations between the second and fourth do not characterise him as a devious speaker – just a passionate one.

*

Oedipus is above all an emotional man, with a very powerful rhetoric of self-conviction which many readers have found persuasive. Yet he is a character, not the voice or mouthpiece of the poet, and so his motives, beliefs and actions are ever under the microscope. Sophocles allows his audience to see the difficulties and inaccuracies in Oedipus' self-justifications and criticisms of others, but these problems inhere in his situation and character. For him to act as a 'reasonable person' by contemporary standards is self-evidently impossible. The next chapter points out why such a quest is out of the question.

5

Oedipus and the Gods

If categories of mortal behaviour seem unable to encapsulate Oedipus, then his relationship with the gods may prove more significant, both because of their manifold participation within the drama, and their guarantee of the human institutions suppliancy and hero cult, through which Oedipus' story will find its resolution.

1. The divine direct

The *OC* presents an excellent example of the subtleties in the tragic sense of the gods. Though no deity appears, if we except the messenger's report of a voice (1626-8), the influence of a divine framework is visible throughout the play.[1] It is felt through the operation of oracles, the immanence of gods within the landscape of Attica, and in the revelation of a guiding divinity directing the action to its end.

A. Oracles

In a very obvious way, Apollo (and behind him Zeus) controls the action through his original oracle (87-95), which guarantees the success of Oedipus' quest in the *OC* as it had guaranteed his parricide and incest in the *OT*.[2] The oracle is one of the most important ways in which divine will is manifest, and its umbrella extends right over Oedipus' life. The first we hear of is delivered by Apollo to Oedipus before his deeds (87-95):

(Phoebus), when he foretold those many evils
said that this would be my rest in a long time,
when I came to the land of my goal, where I should seize
the seat of the dread goddesses and a stranger's welcome,
there I should end my wretched life,

dwelling as a gain to those who received me,
but disaster for those who sent me, who drove me out;
and signs of guarantee of these things would come to me,
either a quake, or some thunderbolt, or the flash of Zeus.

The second is a series which Ismene brought to Oedipus 'when I was being driven from the land' (356). It's not particularly clear what this oracular procession covered, though it must have had something to do with the rights and wrongs of Oedipus' exile.[3] The third is the oracle which Ismene proceeds to report (389-90):

(he says that) you shall be sought by the men there soon
alive and dead, for the sake of their safety.

The resulting totality suggests divine concern for Oedipus' fate, but it does not predetermine or remove the agents' element of choice: they must still act to fulfil those directions. In that regard, Ismene's news is the final key to Oedipus' knowledge about his fate. Indeed, he has an extraordinary amount of information – not only the place of his death, but its signals and the afterlife of his power as well – and the certainty Oedipus derives from it may make him seem a seer-like figure,[4] as he himself may imply when promising the stranger (74):

Everything I say I will say with sight

Yet, as in the *OT*, oracles are a source of information from which Oedipus, among others, draws inferences and makes plans.[5] Oedipus says as much when reacting to Ismene's report (450-4):

But they (sc. Oedipus' sons) will not gain this man as an ally,
nor ever will benefit from this rule over Thebes
come to them; I know this, hearing from this one (Ismene)
the oracle, and understanding the ancient
divine sayings which Phoebus has finally fulfilled for me.

This is not divine sight, for the new oracle had not stated that he must return to Thebes, simply that he 'must be sought' (389-90) by those there, as his power would be decisive in the coming conflict. He has no intention of returning or giving aid to either of his sons. Absent this power, and disaster is to be

expected by both sides. A similar result ensues upon his reali-
sation that his arrival at the Eumenides' grove fulfilled Apollo's
original prediction (96-8):

> Now I realise that there is no way
> that a trusty bird from you did not lead me finally
> to this grove

This is not a seer's reckoning, but the intelligent guess of a man
faced with an obvious conclusion, or at least a conclusion drawn
from Apollo's original information. Similarly his reaction to the
new oracles: Ismene's statement of his power is limited to the
present conflict between Polyneices and Eteocles. Her prediction '[they will suffer] beneath your anger, when they stand at
your tomb' (411) can be read next to her earlier assertion that
'for them your tomb will be heavy if all is not right' (402) and
refers most obviously to the current war, with perhaps an
intimation of future conflicts. Polyneices is similarly focused on
the present (1331-2), while Creon is never given a chance to
state his interpretation. Yet, when Oedipus persuades Theseus
of his utility, the message is now directed *entirely* towards a
future conflict between Thebes and Athens (604-5):

> **Thes**. What suffering do they fear from the oracles?
> **Oed**. That it is necessary they be struck in this land.

This is Oedipus' construction of Ismene's information, but again
hardly second sight. Given Apollo's statement that he would
'dwell as benefit for those who received me, disaster for those
who sent me' (92-3), it is a natural inference that the presence
of his tomb in Athens will have long-term ramifications for
Theban fortunes. Oedipus is certainly a little selective with
his information, but his is an intelligent prognosis about
Theban reactions to his Athenian sojourn, as Creon hints
darkly at strife between the communities (837, 956-9 and esp.
1037).

As Oedipus' interpretations show, oracles work because of
the construction their interpreters place on them, and this is a
lesson already familiar from the *OT*. The irony of Apollo's oracle
is that, whereas it worked in the *OT* through the limitations of
Oedipus' understanding to lead him actually to commit the

crimes he thought to avoid, in the *OC* he will draw the correct
conclusions and achieve all he aims at.

B. Poseidon, Athene – and Zeus

A large part of the gods' role comprises their presence in the
landscape and identity of Athens, and there can be no two gods
whose association is more important for the city than Poseidon
and Athene.[6] Zeus' brother and daughter were supposed to have
competed for the chief honour at Athens, each offering a gift to
the city – Athene the olive tree, Poseidon a salt-water well
(Herodotus 8.55). Though she won and became the city's patron,
his gift was located, together with the 'original' olive, in the
temple of Erechtheus (a legendary king of Athens) on the
Acropolis. As the god of the sea, Poseidon's support was rather
important to the maintenance of the Athenian maritime empire. If Athene represented the most characteristic power behind her city's success, that success depended also on Poseidon's
favour and co-operation.

He was a particularly important deity at Colonus. Here
Thucydides (8.67) locates his sanctuary where in 411 BC the
assembly was summoned by Peisander's supporters (see Chapter 1, pp. 14-16). In honour of the god as *Hippios* ('of horses'),
the Colonan cult had obvious aristocratic connotations because
of its link with the Athenian *hippeis*, though we should not
assume that only aristocrats would have observed the rites
there,[7] and it is prominent in the play: from here Theseus
arrives to aid Oedipus against Creon (887-900), and again when
the thunder presaging Oedipus' death is heard (1491-5); here
also Polyneices makes his supplication (1156-9); and when the
Athenian stranger describes for Oedipus the local deities, Poseidon is the first mentioned (54-5). His precinct is envisaged close
to the play's setting in and near the grove of the Eumenides and,
as a local institution serving to bridge the gap between the
worlds of the stage and the audience, his cult grounds the play's
action firmly in the audience's conception of Attica and its
history.

The depiction of Poseidon and Athene in the famous 'Ode to
Colonus' helps to draw together the temporal span of that
narrative, and his own essential qualities as god of the sea and
of horses, which correspond to his two gifts to Athens in that
first *stasimon* (712-19):

5. Oedipus and the Gods

> O child of Kronos, for you have set
> the city to this boast, lord Poseidon,
> founding in these regions first
> the bridle that restrainer for horses.
> And the well-oared blade, taking wing[8]
> terribly in his dancing,
> leaps to follow the hundred-footed
> daughters of Nereus.

If the cult of Poseidon *Hippios* at Colonus had an aristocratic flavour, its presentation in the *OC* is more subtle. Not that this flavour is absent, for horses are extremely prominent in the *OC*: the deme's eponymous hero is 'Colonus the horseman' (59); the deme itself 'the most powerful halls of this well-horsed land' (668-9); Oedipus' daughters are rescued in a cavalry action, and so on. But Sophocles seeks to draw Poseidon's significance as widely and harmoniously as possible, summarising his favours to the city when describing Athens as 'well-horsed, well-colted, well-sea'd' (711), a run of epithets marrying the qualities of the typically aristocratic cavalry with that of the generally more democratic navy.[9] This is resumed when Theseus describes the Athenian people at Poseidon's altar as 'both unhorsed and horsed' (899), but Poseidon is also thoroughly associated with Athene, who was also worshipped in Colonus with the epithet *Hippia* (Pausanias 1.30.4). Indeed, in the preceding strophe from the above passage, the chorus had praised the olive tree and its guardianship by Zeus 'of the *Moriae*' (sacred olive trees) and 'grey-eyed Athene' (702-6), thus joining the two deities and their favour for the city in the very structure of the song.

The combination is made again in the second *stasimon*, the 'Battle Ode', where the Athenians pursuing Creon's men are 'those who worship / Athene *Hippia* / and the sea god, earth-holder / the dear son of Rhea' (1070-3). Whether we relate it directly to the events of 411 BC or not, this is a vision of Athens as a community at peace with itself, a vision extending beyond a single historical event to ground the opportunities for social harmony in the deep past.[10] Able to receive and protect Oedipus, and so to receive his favour in turn, Athens flourishes because it has been given power and success by the two gods who represent its power and ambition most particularly.

Poseidon and Athene are not the only two Olympians in the

OC. It is a curious fact of extant tragedy that Zeus plays generally a somewhat distant role, particularly when compared with Homeric epic. Though his power and control over the world seems to be taken for granted, its operation is often indirect. This is certainly the case in the *OC*, but the intervention at the end of the play makes one ponder the subtle influence of Zeus over the narrative, and Oedipus' fate in general.

Characters often invoke Zeus at moments of extreme emotional reaction; the chorus cry 'Zeus defender' when they catch sight of Oedipus (143) and 'O Zeus' when he reveals his identity (221). In these and similar cases,[11] an aporetic invocation summons some (usually) unspecified aid, as Antigone's confused 'whither are we to go, O Zeus?' (1749) at the play's end. Zeus is often little more than a distant and unknowable divine power, which seems to humans to make little sense.[12] That they hope for sense is nonetheless understood, as when the chorus invoke him as the guarantor of the coming fight between Theseus' men and Creon's (1079), and characters frequently express wishes and blessings through him, as Oedipus hoping that Theseus be requited for his steadfast behaviour (642), or the chorus praying 'O Zeus, all-leader of the gods, all-seeing, / may you grant' victory to Theseus' band (1085f.).[13]

A faith in his power is particularly clear in those cases where he is linked with another deity in order to reinforce his / her authority. For instance, when Oedipus damns Polyneices, he predicts his son's imminent death with the guarantee 'if indeed ancient-spoken Justice is really seated beside Zeus in ancient custom' (1381-2); or again, when Oedipus expresses his certainty in Apollo's predictions, he links him with his father (623; also 792-3).[14] Indeed, even Athene can be so subordinated, when the chorus speak of 'Zeus of the *Moriae*' (705) as helping her to keep those trees (her gift) safe and sound.[15]

This is obviously a world in which Zeus' interest and activity is assumed, if only indirectly made manifest. But when the thunder presaging his death is heard, its connection with Zeus has been made clear at the play's start, in the relating of the original oracle (94-5):

> and signs of guarantee of these things would come to me,
> either a quake, or some thunderbolt, or *the flash of Zeus*.

Indeed, Zeus is constantly present here. While the chorus cry out for his aid in their fright (1456, 1471, 1485), Oedipus is convinced of the signs' source (as Theseus 1502) and intimation (1460-1), as is the messenger ('and Zeus of the earth[16] thundered' 1606). All this reaches its culmination when Oedipus' apparent delay is castigated by a voice from an unspecified 'god' (1626) (1627-8):

> O Oedipus, you here, you,[17] why do we delay
> to go? Of old truly are your affairs delayed.

Though it is left unclear which god speaks,[18] its function associates it with the authority of Zeus, whether directly or through the mediation of Apollo's oracular guidance (cf. 623 and 792-3). Zeus has caused everything to happen in accordance with his will. The 'god' may be said to be in his heaven, and all is – eventually – right with the world.

C. The Eumenides

The Eumenides ('Kindly Ones') loom large in the *OC*, most obviously in the fact that the play is set in and around their grove.[19] No trace of it remains in Colonus, and Pausanias (second century AD) makes no mention of it (1.30.4), though a roofing tile has been found in Colonus with the inscription 'of the *Semnai Theai*' ('Reverend Goddesses').[20] Pausanias does, however, mention a cult of these *Semnai* on the Areopagus in Athens (1.28.6), where Oedipus was also said to be buried. Though there is much uncertainty here about the historical and mythical relationships of the various cults (see Chapter 3, pp. 41-5), there is a powerful association between Oedipus and the Eumenides throughout the *OC*.[21]

In Athenian myth the Eumenides were known primarily by the title *Semnai Theai*, and eventually came to be identified with the *Erinyes* ('Angry Ones'). In his *Eumenides* (458 BC), Aeschylus had famously identified the avenging Erinyes familiar from Homer with the *Semnai Theai* worshipped on the Areopagus, introducing them into the Athenian community and transforming them from principles of unthinking revenge into socially beneficent figures, without removing their fearful aspect (*Eum.* 932-37, 954f.) but also without ever calling them Eumenides. In the *OC*, Oedipus twice uses of them the term

'Reverend Goddesses' (89-90, 458; cf. 41), so when the Athenian stranger remarks that 'the people here call them / the Eumenides who see all; but other names are good elsewhere' (42-3), immediately after having named them as the 'fearful goddesses ... the daughters of Earth and Darkness (39-40)', an Athenian audience would surely identify Sophocles' Eumenides/*Semnai Theai* with the Erinyes/*Semnai Theai* of Aeschylus, and would therefore appreciate their ambivalent power – to help and harm[22] – within the context of the *OC*.[23]

This ambivalence is clear from the opening of the play, where Antigone's description of the place's natural beauty (16-18) makes a powerful contrast with the fear which both the stranger (36f.) and the chorus (118f.) exhibit at Oedipus' presence there. As simultaneously the 'fearful goddesses' (40) and the 'Kindly Ones' (42), they are obviously suggestive figures in an Oedipal context, for his fate is to 'dwell as benefit for those who received me / and disaster for those who sent me' (92-3), and his desire for revenge is clear throughout the play (see Chapter 7, pp. 121-33). This is well understood by Polyneices (1299; 1432-4):

I say the cause (sc. of Theban strife) is your (sc. Oedipus') Erinys

Don't hold me back; but my concern will be this road, ill-fated and evil, at the hands of our father here and his Erinyes.

He has good reason to think in this way; one critic has even asked 'is it too much to say that Oedipus earns his status as a chthonian power by acting like the unpersuaded Furies of the *Oresteia*?'[24] After all, there have been a multitude of Oedipal curses throughout the play,[25] and to pursue and fulfil curses was the Erinyes' traditional function. Indeed, Oedipus invokes the Eumenides as '*daimones*' ('powers' 864, 1391), so the functional equivalence Polyneices expresses is well represented in the *OC*'s structure and action.

It is reinforced by a series of shared themes and vocabulary: Oedipus' description as 'sober' meeting the 'wineless' deities of the grove (100), for such offerings to the Eumenides were customary;[26] the chorus are as afraid of looking on Oedipus as they are of trespassing on the grove;[27] the chorus term him 'dread to

look on' (141), and he calls the Eumenides 'dread faced' (84); the
poet uses the word *hedrâ* to refer 'not only to Oedipus' seat (36,
45, 112) but also to the seat of the Eumenides (84, 90)';[28]
Theseus also refers to the 'kindliness' of Oedipus (*eumeneian*
631) after the chorus has enjoined Oedipus to pray that, 'as we
call them the Eumenides, let them receive / from kindly
(*eumenôn*) breasts their saving suppliant' (486-7); Oedipus
claims that 'all things seeing will I speak' (*panth' horônta
lexomen* 74) soon after hearing that he is in the grove of the
Eumenides 'who see all' (*tâs panth' horôsas* 42);[29] he later refers
to 'my *alastôr*' (788f.), a term typically and frequently used of
the Erinyes,[30] while predicting his eternal hostility to Thebes;
the Athenian stranger notes Oedipus' presence in the grove
with the same expression ('you hold the area' *ekheis ... khôron*
37; cf. also Theseus at 1768) he then uses to denote its dedica-
tion to the Eumenides (*emphoboi theai sph' ekhousi* 39-40) and
then the larger area's link with Poseidon (*ekhei de nin / semnos
Poseidôn* 54-5), his epithet here linking with the 'holy name' of the
Eumenides themselves (*semnon onoma* 41); and the same
stranger closes his description of Colonus by remarking on the
'dwelling with' (*xunousiai* 63) of its deities, which is precisely what
Oedipus asks for, as Theseus notes, 'you would speak a great gift
from your dwelling with us' (*tês xunousias* 647).

A structural parallel comes in the two rites of supplication /
propitiation, one instructed and performed at the play's beginning, the other instructed and promised at its end. The first
concerns Oedipus' propitiation of the Eumenides (469-92), and
the second Athenian tendance of his hero cult (1518-55).[31] In
each case, Oedipus is involved, first requesting 'instruction'
from the chorus (468, 480), and then giving such 'instruction' to
Theseus (1518, 1539).[32] Prominent in each is his daughters'
cleansing role; in the first scene Ismene has to perform the entire
rite (495-509), in the second Antigone and Ismene bathe their
father and dress him in fresh clothes (1597-1603) – and in both
Sophocles specifies the use of poured water (469-70; 1598-9).

The rites do not share precisely the same purpose: while
Oedipus' cult will ensure aid for Athens in moments of military
necessity (1524-5), his supplication of the Eumenides is to make
him 'pure in the eyes of these *daimones*' (466) for transgressing
their sacred grove. It foreshadows his acceptance by Theseus,
for the chorus' instructions (as with the stranger's (75-80) in-

junction) suggest a support beyond the merely personal desire of an autocratic ruler. Additionally, though this first rite is not an expiation of Oedipus' blood guilt, 'the Erinyes ... are animate agents of pollution who embody the anger of one slain by a kinsman',[33] and so Ismene's performance counterbalances the *miasma* of which the chorus were initially afraid (220-36, 256-7). Oedipus is not directly 'purified', though the chorus speak in these terms (*katharmon* 466) with regard to the Eumenides, he problematically claims this status (287, 548),[34] and it might be suggested by his undressing and bathing at the play's end (1597-1603).[35] Nonetheless, his pollution is 'cancelled out' at the moment of death and translation into a saving hero, but it is not a direct or simple process.

Polyneices' words (1299, 1432-4 above) reveal a tremendous insight into his father. In the most basic terms, Oedipus' Eumenidean aspects prepare for his transformation at the play's end, but the link sources the fundamental paradox of the Eumenides' power – vengeance and benefit – as the key to his own character. When Apollo foretold Oedipus' rest with these goddesses, he knew exactly what he was talking about.

*

The influence of the divine in the *OC* is multifaceted, combining Olympian divinities and their mechanisms with the darker, chthonian ('from the earth') deities. Prepared for at the play's start, where Oedipus asks them to 'be not inconsiderate of Phoebus and me' (86), this interrelationship is sealed in the messenger's speech (1648-55):

> We looked back and saw
> that man (Oedipus) nowhere still present,
> but the lord himself (Theseus) as shade for his eyes
> holding his hand before his face, as though some terrible
> fearsome thing had appeared, unbearable to look on.
> Yet then after a very short space
> *we see him worshipping the ground together*
> *with Olympus, home of the gods, in the same address.*[36]

Theseus' action acknowledges together the gods who have controlled Oedipus' life and those with whom he is to be associated in death. The combination proves not unkind, for there is to be some compensation for Oedipus' terrible suffering, one envisaged even before his career. There is, of course, a limit to that benevolence: it does not extend to Oedipus' family, nor indeed his original community. Divine guidance is hardly benevolent to mankind as a whole, nor does it lead to a Christian reward in the afterlife: instead, Oedipus' compensation is to have the lasting power to revenge himself on his enemies and their descendants.[37] The favour extended to him is the flipside of the ambivalent attitude routinely shown to extraordinary men in tragedy – suffering and honour, often in unequal measure. The next natural question, the system's inherent justice (or lack of it), has proven difficult to answer.[38] Participants often seem to expect this, as the chorus hope in their prayer for Oedipus' easy death (fourth *stasimon*, esp. 1565-7):

> For, after many pains even in vain
> have come upon him,
> once more a *just* (*dikaios*) god would exalt him.

But any answer depends on an interpretation of Oedipus' fate as a suppliant figure and recipient of hero cult, to which we now turn.

2. Saving suppliants and cult heroes

The influence of the gods can also be seen in the human institutions which they are believed to support, and which in turn provide the solutions to the problems of the play. Oedipus is a man of polarised extremes (see Chapter 7, pp. 121-33), perhaps the most important of which is the fact that he is both a suppliant of Athens and its future saviour, as the chorus note in their daring juxtaposition 'the saving suppliant' (*ton hiketên sôtêrion* 487).[39] This duality dominates his fortunes and structures the play, but his character remains the driving force behind the way in which these two elements are joined.

A. Suppliant hero
The *OC*'s story shares a narrative pattern with several other tragedies (Aeschylus' *Suppliant Women*, Euripides' *Suppliant Women* and *Children of Heracles*), the so-called 'suppliant' dramas, in which

the suppliant, in flight from a powerful enemy, seeks refuge in a foreign land. He must win the support of his host, who, when the enemy approaches, undertakes to save him even at the cost of war. The battle ends favourably for the suppliant's cause, and his safety is assured.[40]

Suppliancy was an important institution in the ancient world, although it was by no means automatically granted, and there are several examples of its rejection.[41] Athens even had a guard outside the Acropolis in order to prevent unsuitable figures from claiming asylum.[42] Nonetheless, it was a consistent theme in Athenian self-presentation that the city had always been a refuge for suppliants,[43] and tragedy was one of the great vehicles for expressing pride on this point, with several such dramas set there (aside from the *OC*, the *Children of Heracles* and (Euripides') *Suppliant Women* are the most notable).[44]

In several ways, however, the *OC* is untypical of the type, its variations being directly attributable to its central character. The two most significant are in the way supplication is sought and granted, and its repetition in Polyneices' scene. Supplication is usually a matter of throwing oneself on the mercy of someone else, using the 'expected arguments of kinship, friendship, religious obligation',[45] and applying directly to the person of greatest authority. But Oedipus never makes a formal plea for supplication to Theseus, though he does use conventional themes when speaking to the Athenian stranger and the chorus.[46] Instead, his promised favour to Athens is the crucial element to the success of his supplication.

Indeed, the stranger was so impressed by that promise (70-4) that he advised him to hide in the grove until the local inhabitants decide his case (75-80). The chorus, initially so opposed to his presence (226-36), are won over when Oedipus delivers his first apology, which opens with the famous Athenian reputation (258-64):

> What then of repute, or what benefit is there
> from a fair report flowing in vain,
> if they say that Athens is the most pious,
> that it alone is able to save *xenoi* in ill straits,
> and alone able to protect him?
> And where is this in my case, if you raise me
> from these seats and then drive me out ...

5. Oedipus and the Gods

After the typical justification of his position and past (265-76), he returns to the mutual support of divinity and suppliancy (277-83) before closing with the rather significant rider (287-91):[47]

> For I have come holy and pious and bearing
> benefit to these citizens; and whenever your lord
> arrives, the one who leads you,
> hearing then will you know all; before then
> do not in any way be base.

Just as with the stranger, the mention of civic benefit leads the chorus immediately to defer to those with real authority (294-5):

> But it satisfies me
> that the lords of this land decide these things.

Furthermore, after hearing Ismene's news about *stasis* in Thebes and the new oracle confirming his power, they are even moved to instruct him in a rite to propitiate the Eumenides. Like Theseus, they begin by granting his pitiable state, before returning to the crucial factor (461-4):

> Oedipus, you are worthy of pity,
> you and your children here; *but since to/by this speech*
> *you add yourself as the saviour of this land,*
> *I am willing to advise you ...*

Pity by itself is not enough to guarantee Oedipus' supplication, and neither the stranger nor the chorus are able to grant him permanent shelter. Before Theseus arrives, therefore, Oedipus has not been successful. Though he has deployed (some) suppliant *topoi*, he has gained only the pity and assistance of his interlocutors, and their willingness to leave the crucial decision to another.

It is, therefore, notable that Oedipus does not use supplication themes when speaking to Theseus, who arrives guessing his identity (551-7), eager to know what is required from him and his city (557-60), and full of sympathy (560-6).[48] Oedipus does not throw himself on Theseus' mercy or even ask for shelter, but simply offers himself as a gift (576-8):

77

> I have come to give my wretched body
> to you, a gift not eager to the sight; but the
> gains from it are greater than a fine form.

Theseus' following questions are disbelieving, but after Oedipus relates the Theban desire to get hold of him, and delivers his famous 'time changes all' speech (see Chapter 7, p. 125), the Athenian has all the information he needs and accepts him as a 'citizen' (637).[49] Theseus' first two avowed reasons for doing so – 'an allied hearth' (632-3) and the fact of his suppliancy (634-5) – must be read against the conclusion that 'he brings to this land and to me no small tribute' (635). Politics and pragmatics dominate. Each of the three Athenians to encounter Oedipus – stranger, chorus and Theseus – are persuaded about his utility, whereupon they offer him increasingly effective and important practical assistance.[50]

Nonetheless, they are all based essentially on the fact that Oedipus promises a benefit which, by the time of his interview with the King, has become the entirety of his appeal.[51] This shift away from suppliancy is due to the fact that between speaking to the chorus and meeting Theseus for the first time, Oedipus has had the news from Ismene of the new oracle about the importance of his tomb, which has given a renewed and imme-diate focus to his existence. The whole process of Oedipus' supplication is influenced by his coming hero cult.

The *OC*'s second variation on the supplication pattern lies in the fact that, once Oedipus' is assured and proven, the poet repeats it with Polyneices. We deal elsewhere with general similarities between father and son (Chapter 7, pp. 118-21), but note here the similarity in their suppliant situations. Aside from a shared position and state of dejection, an unfriendly audience is softened up by Antigone (237-53; 1181-1203); the revelation of the suppliant's identity produces revulsion and reluctance to hear him speak (220-36; 1169-78); a reminder to respect suppliancy and the gods is delivered (Oedipus to the chorus 258-65, 277-83; Theseus to Oedipus 1179-80; cf. also Antigone 1183); Polyneices appeals to their common exile (1292-8, 1333-7), a fact which Theseus had earlier invoked as reason for his own sympathy (562-8); and both father (48, 286; cf. also 428) and son (1273-4, 1278) plead that they be not 'dishonoured' (*atim-*) by the supplicated – indeed, Oedipus later rejects his son in these very terms (1378).

These parallels are very significant, given that this second supplication is much more like what we should expect from someone in this circumstance. Polyneices invokes *aidôs* (1268), acknowledges his helplessness without his father's favour (1309-10, 1326-30), emphasises their bond of kinship (1323-4) and the obligations attending suppliant status (1285-8), and justifies his situation (1292-98) – the full run of suppliant *topoi*. However, the sympathy between Theseus and Oedipus (esp. 560-8, 631-5) is lacking between father and son, for all Polyneices' attempts to establish it. By far the most pressing irony is that, having achieved his own success, Oedipus refuses it in another – something which happens 'nowhere else in surviving tragedy'.[52] Of course, that shows the changes in the old man's status, from impotence to power, and it also reminds us that Oedipus succeeded because he had something beyond the mere fact of suppliancy. Polyneices has no such additional resource, and his list of allies (1301-25), for all its practical immediacy, is pathetically material.[53] But in the end, the crucial thing is that Oedipus is no Theseus.

The pattern of suppliant drama shapes the *OC*, and brings out the individuality of Oedipus, who distorts the usual associations and practices of such figures. In order to appreciate how these variations are effected, and what they mean, we turn now to Oedipus' second institutional identity – the cult hero.

B. Saviour in cult(s)

Something belies Oedipus' bedraggled appearance in the *prologos*. This is the promise of ever more specific future benefit,[54] the first clue of which comes when he tells the stranger that 'giving small protection, [Theseus] will gain something great' (72). What that is becomes clear only once the stranger leaves, when Oedipus reveals that Apollo had told him the place of his death, where he would dwell 'as a gain to those who received me, / but disaster for those who sent me, who drove me out' (92-3). This power is then twice repeated before the chorus, in his first apology (287-90), where he speaks of his 'benefit' to the citizens, and then after cursing his sons (421ff.), where he characterises himself as a 'great saviour / for this city, ... but toil for my enemies' (459-60). This second occasion falls after Ismene gives her father and the chorus the significant information that Oedipus' power is to be related to his tomb (402).

Further details are soon forthcoming: Oedipus' 'wretched body' is a 'gift' (575-6) whose benefit is to be found 'in time' (580), when Theseus becomes his 'burier' (582). The importance of the latter fact is to be seen in that Oedipus' 'sleeping and hidden corpse / will one day, cold itself, drink their (Thebans') warm blood' (621-2), and he stays in Colonus because here he 'will have power over those who cast me out' (646). As he tells Theseus, this tomb 'will render for you a strength worth many shields / and the imported spear of neighbours' (1524-5), while the preservation of secrecy will ensure that Theseus 'dwells in this city unravaged / by the sown men' (i.e. Thebans) (1533-4). All these themes – benefit and harm, the power of the tomb, blood-offerings – are obvious references to the important institution of hero cult.

Hero cults were widespread in Attica (and Greece), and they aimed at the propitiation of the powerful dead, whose preternaturality in life – for good or ill – was the reason they were considered so powerful in death.[55] Though heroes familiar from epic poetry and the great Panhellenic myths were so honoured, cults were also conducted for relatively anonymous figures, and (as the Classical period progressed) even for ordinary citizens.[56] Offerings were usually made at the site of the grave, and could include blood, water and even meals which they would 'share' with the living. The purpose of these cults could be viewed narrowly, that is, as getting the hero to aid, or at least not to harm, the person making the offering, but they were also a way of marking the *polis*' territory and giving it some kind of ritual shape. They were certainly a numerous and important articulation of the Athenian landscape, with e.g. the ten tribes (the basic divisions of the population) each having its own 'eponymous' hero.[57] A particularly common type, however, was the local hero whose aid could be invoked against a specific threat to the countryside.[58] Oedipus' cult and its purpose in the *OC* had a myriad of Attic realities to surround it.

Though it is controversial as to how – or how far – hero cult is significant for Athenian tragedy, in some dramas it plays an explicit role.[59] In the *OC* the relationship between a cultic future and the dramatic present is obvious from the very beginning. The bargaining power of Oedipus' person and coming cult distorts or shapes several elements in the suppliant pattern (above), giving him a growing confidence, defining his relationship with Theseus, and contributing to the certainty with which he rejects his son's supplication. But cultic institution and practices can illumine more than this. Oedipus' implacability is evident throughout the play, and this is a common element in cultic narratives, helping to explain the direction, continuities and potency of the hero's attitude after death. This is not to reduce Sophocles' play to some religious aetiology, but to argue that his character makes him suitable for that role. In fact, the extremity and absoluteness of his hatreds, as well as his association with the Eumenides, are fundamentally related to his cultic translation, for they approximate him to the principles and practices of the gods. As a dead hero, Oedipus is not of course divine, but he exercises a power beyond that of ordinary men. Furthermore, the secrecy in which Oedipus wraps both the place and processes of his worship (624-6, 1522-34, 1640-4, 1760-3) is also paralleled by contemporary hero cults, and usually to prevent the wrong people making a claim on the hero's favour.[60]

Reticence in this regard is also a feature of 'mystery' cults, institutions in which the initiates (*mystai*) were specially favoured in life and after death.[61] The most famous of all was the Mysteries of Demeter and Persephone celebrated at Eleusis (*c.* 20 km west-north-west of Athens), which is continually and variously summoned in the *OC*.[62] It is a prominent part of the divine landscape constructed by the chorus in its first and second *stasima* (683, 1050-3); Demeter's temple is also located close to the place where Oedipus goes through his pre-death rituals (1600; cf. below); in its 'liminal' nature, the 'sheer threshold' (*katarraktên odon* 1590) may evoke the grotto at Eleusis where a similar entry to the underworld was located; the 'Thorician stone' (1595) is linked with Thoricus, a deme on the northwest coast of Attica where a cult of Demeter and Persephone was located, and where (*Homeric Hymn to Demeter* 125-6) Demeter (according to her own false tale) enters Attica, which could then be connected with the story of Theseus' descent into the underworld with Peirithous to rape Persephone (1593-4), where Persephone had gone earlier when raped by Hades;[63] Oedipus refers to his recognition of the Eumenides as the 'watchword' of his fate (*xunthêm'* 46), which is picked up later in the 'pledges' of Theseus and Peirithous (*xunthêmata* 1594) near the place where the old man disappears, and may

refer to the 'token' (*sunthêma*) which the initiate to the Mysteries was expected to provide as proof of his readiness for
initiation;[64] Oedipus says that he is led by 'the goddess of the
dead' (1548), and the chorus in the following *stasimon* pray to
Hades and 'the unseen goddess' (1556) (Persephone) to harbour
Oedipus in the underworld. Furthermore, several traditions
outside the *OC* associated Oedipus with Demeter: Androtion
made him a suppliant in her precinct in Colonus, whence Creon
tried to drag him, while Lysimachus located his tomb in Demeter's precinct in Boeotian Eteonos (see Chapter 3, pp. 42-3).

These certainly amount to a powerful complex of references.
Lowell Edmunds has speculated that it reveals Oedipus' original chthonic nature as a vegetation deity, while Claude Calame
(among others) argues that his experience is somewhat like that
of the Eleusinian initiand, who gains access to secret knowledge
and a favoured position in the afterlife.[65] I suspect that allusions to Eleusinian cult perform much the same function as the
OC's allusions to Oedipus' other burial options – to include and
subordinate the association between Demeter and Oedipus in
other traditions to the current story. But even if the audience is
invited to consider Oedipus' life (or death) according to mystery
cult, it need not follow that he is an initiand: allusions can point
out differences as well as similarities. At a minimum, the
mystery nexus helps at a minimum to increase the numinous
and chthonic aura of Oedipus' cult, and to offer an association
with another deity with somewhat contradictory elements, for
Demeter had many chthonian aspects to her worship.[66]

Whether or not Oedipus should be seen as an initiand or a
model for initiands, it should not give the impression that he
undergoes some kind of apotheosis at the end of the play.[67] He
dies (albeit in a rather indeterminate manner),[68] is buried
(though the precise location is unknown), and from the underworld he exercises power over his enemies, and extends
protection over his friends. In this, he is a typical hero.

At the heart of hero cult lies a fundamental reciprocity,
where honours paid are the price for favour, or at least the
avoidance of anger. The nature of these honours is left open:
Oedipus' conception is unsurprisingly rather limited, and the
secrecy of his tomb site (aside from its mythological advantages:
see Chapter 3, pp. 41-5) seems to demand that no honours are
to be paid there; instead of the usual libations, he shall receive

the 'warm blood' of his enemies (621-3). None of this means that honour could not be paid to him in other ways, nor that the notion of his saving presence in Athens, as a subject of commemoration, is not in itself an honour (as he hints to Theseus (1555): 'may you, fortunate always, make remembrance of me in death'). Oedipus' conception need not fix the form and function of his cult, though it is quite fitting that he should try to do so,[69] for one cannot transfer stage rituals directly onto the world of the audience.[70]

The language of reciprocity (*kharis* 'favour') is very prominent,[71] and its polysemic repetition expresses the continuities between Oedipus' behaviour in life and his power in death. His familial relationships are described by the presence (1106) or absence (767, 779) of this quality, in accordance with which he has an absolute tendency to repay good and bad (see Chapter 7, pp. 121-33). Perhaps Oedipus' most striking – and revealing – statement of its power is negative, and it comes when answering Creon's first attempt at persuading him to return to Thebes (775f.), as he asserts vehemently that an unwanted or untimely *kharis* is in fact no *kharis* at all.

This imperative is repeated in a political context, *kharis* describing the assistance rendered Oedipus by Theseus and Athens (586) as well as the benefit he wishes to repay (636-7, 1489-90, 1498), but its final expression moves the audience entirely to the otherworld (1751-3):

Thes. Cease lamentation, children. For one must not weep
where there is stored a common[72] *kharis*
from the earth; for (it would cause) divine anger.

This favour, as Oedipus had promised Theseus (1518-19), is now shared for the entire community's benefit (*xun'* 'common' 1752) through his permanent cult. The responsibility for its maintenance falls to Theseus, who must pass on the secrets in an unbroken line to the city's rulers (625-6, 1530-4). Though this might suggest uncertainty over its continuity to the democratic city, the Areopagus council was particularly considered the guardian of the city's 'secret deposits / tombs'.[73] Given even Theseus' uncertain reputation in these terms,[74] perhaps the notion of indirect succession actually helps to guarantee continuity, and produces the developmental wiggle-room required for the cult's evolution between the play's setting and the audience's present.

In those terms, it is surely significant that Theseus speaks from a community perspective when he stops Antigone and Ismene from fulfilling their family duty – lamentation over the dead – explicitly because of the 'common benefit' Oedipus will bring. In this way the interests of Laius' polluted and doomed house become secondary to those of the Athenian community. This was foreshadowed by the messenger describing Oedipus' death as 'marvellous' and 'not with grieving' (*ou stenaktos* 1663), but also in the perverted performance of Oedipus' death ritual. He removes his clothes, is washed and dressed once more by his daughters (1597-1605) – all typical funeral actions, though falling *before* his death, from which he excludes his family (1640-4; cf. also 1528-9). Partially this inversion is due to the fact that his body is to disappear, its precise whereabouts unknown or a matter of contention. Certainly this is not the only way in which his death is unusual – foretold him many years ago, heralded by Zeus' thunder, signalled by a divine voice, achieved with a blinding vision, shrouded in mystery[75] – so one might contend that the communal element in the exclusion of Ismene and Antigone, or in the whole play, is perhaps overstressed. Nonetheless, if Oedipus spends much of the play cutting himself off from his family and original community, this final moment sets the seal on his translation from private individual to public property.[76] The miraculous elements do not detract from this progression; instead, they make the promise of his future power as a hero seem all the greater, represented as it is by the many divine signals of his exceptionality in life.

This is the point of hero cult in tragedy: characters who are somehow more than human in their achievements and failures can, for all their destructiveness in life, become after death something useful and socially beneficial. It is one of the structured, institutionalised ways in which the gap between the worlds of the play and the audience may be bridged, illustrating to the latter where they have come from; that is, both how they differ from, and in what ways they represent an improvement upon, that heroic world. His death is an ending point in the world of heroes – not *the* ending point of that world, of course – and one from which institutional and social development may be traced. Thus do the gods justify the chorus' hope that a

5. Oedipus and the Gods

dikaios daimôn would raise Oedipus up (1565-7), or Ismene's belief that the new oracle shows how the gods are 'setting him upright' (394). The conflicts coalescing in Oedipus' person, sourced from his birth, his character and his (pre)history cannot be resolved within his lifetime, or that of any mortal like him. Yet the power of these extraordinary beings is not lost; it is translated. In this way is the divinity *dikaios* both to the implacable nature of the hero and the needs of human society. Though the historical realities may have suggested otherwise to some members of the audience (and some modern critics),[77] Sophocles' vision of Athens – at least for saving and then being saved by Oedipus – is ultimately reassuring.[78]

*

The *OC* has been deemed 'episodic',[79] but its structure is in fact integrated and complex. The first of its two basic 'institutional' constituents is the suppliant process: the traditional sequence (reception, threat and resolution) dominates the play's first three episodes, whereafter another supplication process is begun in the fourth, but swiftly abandoned. It is at this point, with the departure of Polyneices, that the second of the *OC*'s constituents – hero cult – takes over entirely, though it has made its presence felt from the opening of the play in Oedipus' first announcement of the old oracle; in Ismene's confirmation of that message; in subtle changes enacted in Oedipus' supplication strategies; and in his implacable furies. Indeed, although the play's structural dynamic consists of the interaction between supplication and hero cult, the *OC* is neither a simple suppliant drama, nor a mere cultic narrative. But the way in which its constituents are interlocked is only a partial explanation for the poet's success in these terms. Between these imperatives sits Oedipus himself, and it is his character, his story, which shapes them and binds them together.

6

Athens and Attica

The last chapter revealed that the *OC*'s structure moves attention from Oedipus himself to the socialised and divinely guaranteed ways in which his conundra will be resolved. This chapter places these solutions in a larger social and dramatic context, considering both the chorus' role and relationship with the Athenian polity, and then the function of the territory itself.

1. Chorus and community

The chorus of Athenian tragedy is difficult for a modern audience to comprehend.[1] Twelve or fifteen members in number,[2] they enter the orchestra after the *prologos*, and remain there until the play's end (exits within the drama are very rare in extant tragedy). They interact with the characters, mark the major pauses between arrivals and departures with separate songs (*stasima*), and provide another perspective, and source of commentary, on the action. Their singing is separated formally from the spoken or chanted utterances of the main characters, delivered in a different dialect from the Attic which dominates the dialogue, and more poetic in its language and syntax. Of course, characters may sing (as, e.g., 237-53) and, when the chorus engages in dialogue (as, e.g., 254-7, 461-509), its leader steps forward to do so. The boundaries between character and chorus are permeable. Against the earlier fashion to interpret their words as those of the poet or an ideal spectator, most critics now see theirs as simply another perspective, as limited by dramatic identity as the characters themselves. They should be viewed not as a separate character or even a group of such characters, but first and foremost a group within a world dominated by individuals.

6. Athens and Attica

The significance of that fact can only be seen when we remember that choruses were drawn solely from Athenian citizens, and that choral singing and dancing was not only a central form of religious worship (after all, tragedies were performed at a festival to the god Dionysus), but even an essential marker of Greek education, culture and civilisation.[3] Almost every male audience member would have performed in such a chorus, and very many in the same theatre of Dionysus. Yet the chorus does not simply mirror the audience's values, or provide a 'democratic' participant in an heroic world: for one, they are generally ineffective in preventing or substantially influencing the individually driven disasters on stage,[4] and they usually comprise those who are not straightforwardly representative 'citizens': young women, old men, and so on. Yet they are a source of identification and continuity – and difference – helping the audience locate and understand the dynamics structuring the heroic world. In short, the chorus is a group whose views the audience is invited to ponder as those of a group, but not as the only, or even the best, such reaction.

Their importance may also be seen in the amount of their lyric dialogue (*amoibaion*) with the actors. The *OC* uses more *amoibaion* than any other Sophoclean play, and its chorus is more involved in the action than most other extant choruses.[5] This is reflected in the play's structure: the chorus not only mark episode breaks with *stasima*, but also pauses within the episodes through exchanges with the characters, revealing a typical progression of (a) character dialogue, (b) lyric dialogue, (c) character dialogue, (d) *stasimon* thus:

prologos (1-116)
parodos (117-253)

1st episode A (254-509)	3rd episode (1096-1210)
amoibaion (510-48)	
1st episode B (549-667)	
1st *stasimon* (668-719)	3rd *stasimon* (1211-48)
2nd episode A (720-832)	4th episode A (1249-1446)
amoibaion (833-86)	*amoibiaon* (1447-1504)
2nd episode B (887-1043)	4th episode B (1505-55)
2nd *stasimon* (1044-95)	4th *stasimon* (1556-78)

87

exodos A (1579-1669)
kommos (1670-1750)
exodos B (1751-79)

Aside from the third episode (Oedipus' reunion with his daughters and the announcement of Polyneices' arrival), this map makes clear the frequency and thoroughness of choral participation. This is obvious from the dynamic *parodos*, when the chorus burst in looking for the intruder and conduct a dialogue with Oedipus and Antigone to reveal their identity. A similar dynamism is evident also in their *amoibaion* with Creon and Oedipus in the second episode (833-86), where the emotionally heightened singing conveys the interchanges as Creon drags off Antigone and then tries to do the same to Oedipus. Though choreography cannot be reconstructed, there could well be some movement towards Creon, for he tells them to 'keep back' (836) and 'not to touch him' (865). Both exchanges also show a superficially active and authoritative chorus unable to prevent Creon's designs without the aid of Theseus himself.[6] In the *parodos*, for instance, their initial insistence on removing Oedipus (156f., 176f., 220-36) founders upon his self-defence and promise of aid (288-95):

> **Oed**. *When some man of authority*
> *appears, he who is the leader of you,*
> *then hearing you will know all*; but in the
> meanwhile in no way become bad.
> **Ch**. Old man, there is much need to
> have respect for your thoughts; for they are
> named in words not short; *I am satisfied*
> *that the lords of this land should determine these things.*

That change of heart describes Theseus in such terms (297-8, 301, 303-7) as to represent their utter conviction in his authority. Similarly, despite the charge of protection Theseus lays on the chorus (638, 653) – he closes the scene by claiming that 'his name' shall protect Oedipus (667) – they cannot stop Creon from realising his intentions and have to summon Theseus (841-3, 884-6). Partly this is down to old age, emphasised from the very beginning of the play (112 and often) and mentioned by them at the moment of crisis as Creon arrives (726-7), but it has also another purpose in the play. The effect of the third *stasimon* about the difficulties of life is considerably enhanced by the singers' age, while the sympathy between the chorus and Oedipus on the basis of their age is continually emphasised.[7]

Indeed, though eventually unequal to the task, the chorus is placed at the centre of the action until Theseus' second appearance: they are entrusted with the care of Oedipus, struggle with Creon, support Oedipus' first plea to Theseus (629-30), confirm his refutation of Creon (1014-15) and give Polyneices his marching orders (1397-8): in some ways 'a kind of citizen jury'.[8] As one of the three Athenian figures Oedipus encounters, their consent to leave the decision to Theseus, and to assist Oedipus in the Eumenides' rite (466-509), represents a significant narrative stage in his reception, but also a breadth of support for Oedipus' presence in Athenian territory which is not merely social but, as they combine Colonan and Athenian identities, territorial as well. Although their power is not determinative, the old men of the chorus do carry weight in the *OC*'s world.

Their part in his reception affords Oedipus the opportunity for his first two apologies, the first directly after the *parodos* (258-74), the second during the *amoibaion* (510-48) after Ismene brings news of the new oracle (Chapter 4, pp. 53-6). They play little role in the former, for his defence is contained in a contiguous speech, so we concentrate here on the latter passage. Somewhat prurient in their interest for details here, and unafraid to deploy their recently exhibited favour (518, 520) in order to make him speak, the way they draw Oedipus out is a good example of the choral involvement so praised by Aristotle (*Poetics* 1456a25-32), and exhibits another form of 'realism' (if we can use such a term) in Sophocles' technique. Not only does the chorus act like an interested group, but Oedipus is not able to give a formal defence, instead giving them control over the revelation of his sexual misconduct (an issue causing him some discomfort).[9] This rather difficult matter was almost entirely absent from his first apology, so now he is forced to speak by their 'relentless cross-examination'[10] as much as their favour to him.

A similar realism is also clear when, after Polyneices' exit, the chorus react to the thunderclaps heralding Oedipus' doom. In contrast to Oedipus, certain about both the signs' source and import, the chorus are terrified, calling repeatedly to Zeus (1456, 1471, 1485) and confessing their fear (1464-6, 1469), though they do finally join in Oedipus' calls for Theseus (1491-

9), even echoing his reminder (1489-90) of benefit to Athens
(1496-8). Aside from the contrastive purpose (furthered by the
fact that they are singing, while Oedipus is speaking in iambics:
see Chapter 2, pp. 34-5), which helps to underline his individuality and superior understanding, the chorus also expresses
some conventional fear and uncertainty in the face of meteoro-
logical disturbance (as Theseus notes 1500-4), and attributing
it to the divine. This even makes them remember their earlier
horror at the thought of Oedipus' presence in Athens (235-6,
256-7), when they pray 'nor, because I have seen a terrible man
(sc. Oedipus), may I have somehow a return without benefit'
(1483-4), their perturbation highlighted by the increasing level of
(emotive) dochmiac rhythm in their lyrics (Chapter 2, pp. 34-5).

In fact, a desire to avoid divine wrath is characteristic of the
chorus.[11] Their original perturbation over Oedipus' trespass in
the grove is explicitly so sourced (129-33), while their atten-
dance of the Eumenides motivates their aid to Oedipus
(466-509) to seek forgiveness for his transgression. Even then,
they are still tentative (490-2):

> And if you
> were to do these things, I would bravely stand by you,
> but otherwise I would be fearful, o stranger, about you.

Such a caution also informs their many gnomic utterances
during the play: in their final lyric dialogue, the *kommos* with
Antigone and Ismene (1670-1750), they urge Oedipus' daughters 'to endure well that which comes from god' (1694) and 'leave
off this grief; no one is untaken by evils' (1722-3), resuming that
with their final instruction at the very end of the play (1777-9):

> But cease nor rouse to
> greater lamentation;
> for totally have these things their authority.[12]

But the *stasima* show most clearly the chorus' relationship to
the divine, and their place within the world of the drama. There
are four *stasima* in the *OC*, coming at focal points within the
narrative: after Oedipus' reception by Theseus (1. the 'Ode to
Colonus') and before the appearance of Creon; after Creon's
abduction of Ismene and Antigone (2. the 'Battle Ode') and

before the Athenian victory; after the reunion (3. on old age) and before Polyneices' appearance; and after the departure of Oedipus and Theseus (4. a prayer for Oedipus' painless death) but before the messenger's news of the Theban's death. Tragic *stasima* are often scrutinised for lack of relevance to the immediate context, but in some ways that is precisely their point. Their words amplify the action, inviting the audience to consider parallels with other stories, ethical questions or the gods' role, and so completely to contextualise the current story. The effect of their singing on one level is to pause the action so that the audience can reflect on what has come, and ponder what is to come, but *stasima* also encourage interpretation within the progressing performance, and the connection with their surrounds is never simple.

Consider the fourth *stasimon*, the prayer for Oedipus' quick and painless death (1556-78).[13] As with the third *stasimon* (see below), the chorus slightly seem to miss the point, for the point of Oedipus' death is the power it is going to give him. The manner of his passing is, at least for Oedipus himself, a secondary consideration. Divided into two sections, the singing begins with a typical hint of caution, as the chorus open their prayer with hesitation (1556-60):

> If it is right for me to honour the unseen goddess (= Persephone)[14]
> and you with my prayers,
> lord of those in darkness, Aidoneus (= Hades),
> Aidoneus, I pray ...

They continue to ask for Oedipus' painless end, for his sufferings warrant a restoration to honour and power by a 'just *daimon*' (1567), and their accompanying statement, 'after many pains even in vain coming upon him' (1565-6), shows the limitations of their understanding. The antistrophe is also a prayer for the same purpose, this time to the 'goddesses of the earth' (probably the Eumenides themselves)[15] as well as the very rarely invoked and here unnamed Cerberus. They stress Oedipus' status as 'stranger' (*xenos*) (1562, 1577) among the dead, whose 'many-strangered' gates are guarded by Cerberus (1569-70).[16] Beyond the alignment of the chorus' sympathies here, their concern for his reception underlines how far Oedipus has come, from 'stateless' exile (*apoptolis* 208) to a citizen of Athens (*empolin* 637), for they now wish that his successful reception in Athens may be repeated in the underworld. Their prayer links more closely his past and future receptions to underline the reality – and direction – of his cult (Chapter 5, pp. 79-85), but it also prepares directly for the messenger's speech, since their hope is borne out in his story of Oedipus' numinous passage.

The propensity of tragic *stasima* to reach beyond their immediate context is also evident even when the song's substance is intimately related to the dramatic action, as in the 'Battle Ode' (second *stasimon*) (1044-95).[17] Here the chorus imagine themselves participating in the pursuit and struggle with the Thebans, closing with a prayer directed to several deities (Zeus, Athene, Apollo and Artemis) to grant Athenian success. This is described with the language of the hunt (1088-9, 1091), so it is appropriate that they describe Attica's topography in the first strophic pair (1044-73), imagining the two routes the Thebans might take through Athenian territory (1047-53; 1059-61):

> either at the Pythian
> or torch-lit shores,
> where the queenly goddesses nurse the solemn rites
> for mortals, for which a gold
> key stands on the tongue
> of the attendant Eumolpidai
>
> or they approach the west
> of the snowy rock
> from the pasture of Oea.

There is some uncertainty about the precise geography, but the places are obviously meaningful for a contemporary audience. The description is only one in a series in the *OC*, and this *stasimon* broadens the topographical focus of the first *stasimon* ('Ode to Colonus') beyond the environs of Colonus and the Acropolis in Athens (see below).[18] The first two places are denoted by reference to a deity: 'the Pythian shore' (1048) probably refers to Apollo's temple on the bay of Eleusis, while references to the 'queenly goddesses' and the 'Eumolpidai' (an Athenian clan with a prominent role in the cult) invoke Eleusis itself and its Mysteries.[19] Geography is prominently linked with its deities, whose presence is another sign of Athenian favour. This will be manifest in the coming conflict, which will eventuate in Theban defeat pictured in overwhelmingly cavalric terms (1067-70) to augment their description as those 'who honour / Athene *Hippia* / and the sea god, earth holder, / dear son of Rhea (Poseidon)' (1070-3). With many parallels between the land and its supporting deities, the Thebans are facing a hopeless task.

Yet, while moving the narrative focus well beyond the setting of the play, these descriptions also create a vivid sense of the contemporary offstage action, furthered by a rather feverish 'do they act, or are they about to?' (1074) amid their longing to attend the fight or simply see it (as doves! – curiously unwarlike, underlining their helplessness) (1081-2). The chorus and audience become closer in their imagining of the conflict, as indeed in their shared interest in the topography and significance of Attica. As a prediction (cf. esp. 1075, 1079-80) of Athenian success immediately fulfilled, the song is a powerful statement of community power, justifying the city's image and promise in the matching first *stasimon* (668-719), delivered before Creon's arrival. But the connection between these two songs is not merely thematic, for both are set in the middle of a recurrent pattern of (a) promise – (b) affirmation – (c) demonstration. Just as the first *stasimon* praised Athens after (a) Theseus had accepted Oedipus into the community and assured him of his safety, and was followed (c) by its successful testing in resolving to face Creon (cf. esp. 720-1), so the Battle Ode falls after (a) Theseus promises to return with the proof of that assurance, and heralds (c) the successful demonstration of that determination.

As with the Battle Ode, the Ode to Colonus reveals a keen interest in Attica's land, but again with particular emphasis on its inhabiting gods, introducing the scene (668-70):

> Stranger, you have come to the *most powerful homes*
> *of this well-horsed land,*
> that famous gleaming white Colonus, where ...

This description of Attica and Colonus immediately summons the local cult of Poseidon and Athene *Hippia*, and prepares for the focal transfer from Colonus to Athens in the second strophic pair (below).[20] In this first pair (668-93), the vegetation description is always linked to a god: the 'clear voiced nightingale' (671-3; cf. Antigone's opening description 16-18) holds the ivy and the vine, symbols of Dionysus, who honours the deme always with his presence (679-81). Given what it holds, we may suspect a poetic self-reference in the nightingale, for this bird had long been a poetic symbol.[21]

The antistrophe opens with the narcissus 'blooming under divine dew' (681) and the 'crocus golden-rayed' (685). Both plants are particularly associated with 'the great twin goddesses' (683-4), Demeter and Persephone, the former being the plant Persephone was picking when she was raped by Hades, the latter (also picked by Persephone) because women dressed in crocus-dyed robes at one of Demeter's most important festivals, the Thesmophoria.[22] Persephone's rape leads (in some versions) to the grant of cultivation to Athens, and (more commonly) to the Eleusinian Mysteries (see Chapter 5, pp. 79-85), and so these floral allusions herald the divine presence and favour in the second strophic pair, as well as the prominence of Eleusis in the geographical descriptions of the Battle Ode. Fertile land needs water, and the poet naturally moves into praising the Cephisus river (685-91), which ran very close to Colonus but was also famous as 'the' Athenian river in Attic poetry. Sophocles closes this catalogue with the affection shown by the Muses and Aphrodite too, which may have intertextual overtones (Euripides *Medea* 830-45, where the poet places the birth of the Muses in Attica, while Aphrodite sits at the banks of the river Cephisus itself)[23] that reinforce the deeply numinous sense of Athenian geography.[24]

Vitality and permanence dominate the image of Colonus in this first pair, forming a powerful contrast to the principles of time and change enunciated by Oedipus in his immediately preceding speech (607-28):[25] glades are 'green' (673), the vine is 'countlessly fruited' (676); Dionysus 'always' throngs the area (679-80); the narcissus blooms 'every day always' (681-3); the river's fountains are 'without sleep' and flow 'always in the day' (685-6, 688-9). The pairing helps to collapse the temporal distances between the mythical past before the play (inherent in the myths of Eleusis and divine gifts to Athens in the second strophic pair) with both the dramatic and audience's present.

These two themes are also used to make the transition to the song's second strophic pair, which moves away from Colonus to praising the twin sources of more general Athenian strength – the olive representing Athene's support, and from Poseidon the

94

bridle and their maritime pre-eminence. The gifts are as permanent as the first pair's flourishing vegetation: the olive 'blooms' (700), it never grows old nor is destroyed (702-3) because Morian[26] Zeus and Athene are 'ever' (704) vigilant. The original gifts are a permanent boon. It is worth noting, once more, that the harm to Athenian agriculture done during the Decelean War has been overestimated;[27] Sophocles' depiction of the flourishing olive is no mere fantasy.

Once more an elision between Colonus and Athens is the poet's purpose, for the first of Poseidon's gifts is said to have been given 'on these roads first' (715), while the olive and the well of sea water were located on the Acropolis. Each of these has a broader application as well, for the olive was extensively cultivated in Attica, and Athenian domination over the sea extended well into the Aegean. Furthermore, Pausanias (1.30.4) relates the story of an olive tree springing up in the Academy, near Colonus. If his description and the cult is not influenced by the *OC*, then we have another allusion to both local and regional phenomena (see Chapter 3, pp. 41-5). Further intimation comes from the description of Athens as 'well-horsed (resuming the theme from the opening of the *stasimon*), well-colted, well-sea'd' (711), foregrounding Poseidon without neglecting Athene *Hippia* familiar at Colonus. Each allotted one unit in the strophic pair, these two deities look forward to the Battle Ode, where their combined worship will define the Athenians (1070-3). Similarly definitive is the olive tree (694-5):

> There is here something I never hear of in the land of Asia,
> nor ever in the great Dorian island of Pelops ...

This cannot fail to have struck its audience as a particularly convinced statement of their uniqueness, next to their famous Persian foes from the start of the century and the Spartan-led ones at its end. Yet that sense of self-belief is not simplistically 'democratic', for the matching gifts of Poseidon (bridle and oar) unite the cavalry and the navy as the twin manifestations of the god's favour (Chapter 5, pp. 68-9), and link them without subordination to the olive of Athene. Democrat and aristocrat, navy and cavalry – all under Athens' banner.

This famous song looks back to the *polis*' earliest days through one of its foundation myths, but also into the contem-

porary world (and beyond) in the description of the landscape and
its inhabiting deities. The favour of these deities, past, present and
future, guarantees the city's survival and glory. The song's immediate purpose within the play, to inform Oedipus of the power and
beauty of the land to which he has just come, sits well with these
broader effects, and perfectly illustrates the multivalence of ancient Greek choral song. In keeping with the triumphant tone of
its narrative surroundings (for Theseus has just accepted Oedipus
and pledged his protection), Sophocles constructs here a beautiful,
subtle and awesome image of Athenian grandeur and power; it is
no wonder that later ages saw this portion of the *OC* as his own
apology (Chapter 1, pp. 12-13).

A chorus needs neither divine gifts nor mythical narratives
to address broader questions. In the short third *stasimon* (1221-
48), as Theseus leaves the stage to fetch Polyneices, the chorus
ponder the miseries of life and the difficulties of old age, comparing themselves and Oedipus to a headland buffeted from all
directions. Their pessimistic reflections, greatly reinforced by
their own age, begin with a denigration specifically of that fact,
which no one should desire (1211-14), for pains increase as joys
decrease and death comes to all, death 'without wedding hymn,
/ without lyre, without dancing' (1221-2). Of course, the link
with Oedipus' case is at this stage only inferential, to be made
explicit in the epode (1239f.), but the play's consistent emphasis
on Oedipus' old age and its consequent ills (cf., e.g., 1209)
naturally invite the comparison.

The antistrophe continues the hint, expanding the misery to
cover life's entirety (1224-38):

Not to be borne conquers
every reckoning; but, when he appears,
to go thither, from where
he has come, as quickly as possible is by far second.
As when youth is past,
bearing its light foolishness,
what blow of much toil is alien?
What calamity is lacking?
Murder, *stasis*, strife, battles
and envy; and he has as his lot the blamed
final unmixed unsociable
unfriended old age, where all the ills
coming from ills dwell together.

Though the chorus return once more to old age with an astonishing run of asyndetic adjectives (1235-8), their vision of life is a joyless one. Even if the description of youth is positive ('bearing its light foolishness' 1230) – far from certain, as the words are ambiguous – the suitability of these themes to Oedipus' fortunes is very notable: 'murder, *stasis*, strife, battles / envy' (1234-5) could sum up his life, and the lives of his kin, without much further ado. The lesson to be drawn from Oedipus indeed seems to lie at the heart of this apparent digression into platitude, and it is one redolent of a similar lesson in the *OT* (1186-1222), where the chorus found the example of Oedipus too much for humanity to bear. Scholars have focused, often with surprise, on the way that the *OC*'s third stasimon seems to jar with the narrative around it, where Oedipus' daughters have just been restored to him, his death in Athens and honour is assured, his future in cult secure. The usual conclusion is that the chorus here is wrong, or else that Sophocles has simply succumbed to the increasing tendency in late fifth century tragedy for *stasima* having only the loosest of connections with its dramatic surrounds. After all, the chorus do not possess Oedipus' knowledge or certainty about his fate, and they are later terrified by its harbingers (1446ff.).

Yet they're not so wrong about the principles involved. Surely the experience and character of Oedipus, if generalised, *does* lead to this type of suffering – a youth of 'foolishness' followed by a litany of aged woe. Though Oedipus himself may be about to shake off the coil (justifying the chorus' characterisation of death as a 'helper' 1220), neither his daughters, his sons, nor his original community are free from his attendant ills. This point is about to be made in the immediately ensuing encounter with Polyneices, and one should not forget the way in which this *stasimon* foreshadows the behaviour of Oedipus specifically in that scene: *stasis* and 'strife' come to him for adjudication, battles and murder he both predicts and bemoans (at 1361 he even calls his son his 'murderer'), though it is Polyneices' role to express 'envy' at his brother's power (1338-9).[28]

In all these ways, it seems clear that the chorus speak beyond the world of the play directly to the contemporary audience, who imbibe the lesson of Oedipus' extremity, violence and position. As discussed earlier, the tragic hero is not someone you want to have as a neighbour or leader, or marry your daughter to: he is someone whose numinous presence in death is directly linked with his a- or supra-social tendencies in life. While the third *stasimon* presents a different interpretative challenge to that of the other songs, it can be related to the famous second *stasimon* in the *OT* (863-910), where the chorus ponder the 'tyrant's' fate and relationship to 'hybris'.[29] As with the *OC*'s third *stasimon*, scholars have been puzzled by the term's use and the entire discussion, given the generally 'positive' characterisation of Oedipus in that play. But an autocrat in tragedy is an autocrat still: mostly good or thoroughly bad, they provide a lesson, and it is one the choruses in both plays help to convey with a little creative anachronism, by stepping almost out of their dramatic role.

This ambiguity does not, of course, prevent them pitying Oedipus, as they do at the opening of the epode (1239) before comparing him to a headland buffeted in winter from all four directions (1245-8) by 'disasters' (*âtai* 1244), a word which conveys not only troubles inflicted from outside, but those brought on by our own shortcomings. Even pity cannot blind them to the complications and problems of being Oedipus.

The chorus in the *OC* extends the audience's appreciation of the play in several directions. It moves the dramatic focus backwards and forwards, zooms between past and present, and provides ethical and moral commentary to the action. This flexibility prevents us from viewing them as characters, or consistent psychological entities, but it is the key to understanding their role in the drama. At one moment fully involved in the action, at the next moving away from it and closer to the audience, or retreating into the certainties of divine immanence, the chorus in this play reflects all the possibilities and complexities of Greek choral song.

2. Colonus and Athens

Setting is arguably more important to the *OC* than any other extant Attic tragedy,[30] and we have already mentioned it from several angles: as Sophocles' own deme, the *locus* of the oligarchic assembly in 411 BC, Athens' mythical double. The play's emphasis on its locality is evident from the *prologos*, which establishes the two most important themes in the treatment of Colonus: its numinousness and relationship with Athens.

In response to Oedipus' opening question ('to what | lands

have we come, or the city of which men?' 1-2), Antigone answers
(14-18):

> The towers which
> crown the city, as far as I can see, are far off.
> But this place is sacred, so one can guess clearly, teeming
> with laurel, olive and the vine; and thick-feathered
> nightingales sing[31] throughout its interior;

The reply makes a firm distinction between the two places:
Athens (19) can be observed, 'this place' is separate and holy.
While she is only describing the grove of the Eumenides itself,
the geographical separation implicitly extends its sanctity to
the whole of the deme. Her phrasing ('this [is the] place') is
repeated at several points throughout the play, Oedipus twice
asking the same question of the stranger (38, 52) before the
latter confirms Antigone's impression in these terms (54), but it
culminates in Oedipus' confirmation that 'this is the place … in
which I will have power over those who threw me out' (644; cf. 646).
The deme's blanket sanctity is even clearer when the stranger
says Poseidon 'holds' the place (see Chapter 5, pp. 72-3).

Yet topographical specificity is always qualified.[32] Even in
basic terminology, the word *polis* ('city') may denote either the
deme or Athens itself, so the stranger's reticence to do anything
in Oedipus' case 'apart from the city' (47) may refer to either, as
may the chorus' first injunction to Oedipus to depart 'lest you
fasten some further debt on my city' (236). A positive relationship with Athens is established early, the stranger terming
Colonus 'brazen-foot threshold, / the stay of Athens' (57-8) even
while maintaining the inhabitants' separateness under the
name of the local hero Colonus (59f.). He acknowledges that
'these matters are ruled by the King in the city' (67), whose
presence is immediately deemed by Oedipus vital for the supplication process – an exchange mirrored by the chorus'
description of Theseus' overlordship (296-309). In keeping with
the deme's separate identity, the stranger consents only to
summon local people ('the demesmen here in this place, not the
ones in the city' 78) for the decision. They – the chorus – then
enter and demand Oedipus' removal first from the grove and
then from the territory of Athens, speaking with authority and
autonomy. But when the city-wide nature of Oedipus' benefit

becomes clear (287-90), they defer the question to Theseus. Partially this reflects their choral nature, but also the subordination of their political identity to the urban centre. Represented in the chorus' uncertain identity (cf. above), this blurring between the two locations continues when they praise Colonus and Athens in the first *stasimon*, emphasising not only the locale's special qualities, but including the city within their focus. This goes beyond the apparent division of deme and city in the song's structure, where the first strophic pair (668-93) refers mostly to the former, the second (694-719) to the latter, the 'mother city' (707), for the line between this *stasimon*'s elements is not so clear cut: the deities in the first strophic pair are also honoured in Athens, while the eulogy of Athene's olive and Poseidon as tamer of horses look to Antigone's opening description of the grove ('teeming with ... olive' 16-17) and the prominence of Poseidon's cult – and the *hippeis*, of course – at Colonus.

This bivalence is also evident in the duplication, sharing, or simple transference of cults and deities between the two locales, bringing out the second quality of Colonus and Athens, numinousness. Antigone's opening description of the grove's vegetation – the laurel, olive and vine – alluded to the deities whose symbols they represent – Apollo, Athene and Dionysus – before the stranger expands on that impression of divine presence by invoking Poseidon, Prometheus, and the hero Colonus. The catalogue's impression of a pervasive divinity is reaffirmed in the first *stasimon*'s picture of divine immanence, in which, aside from the images of local fertility and cultic power, Colonus is constantly linked with Athens: Poseidon and Athene are present in Colonus, but their gifts resound throughout Attica and the empire, and are represented in the temple of Erechtheus on the Acropolis.

Duplication of this sort is a fundamental element to the play. The very fact that Oedipus' cult was (probably) observed in both places is matched by the twin cults of the *Semnai Theai*, or the Colonan temple of Demeter *Euchlous* and its Areopagite sister to Demeter *Chlous*.[33] Whether this Sophoclean presentation actually matches contemporary reality or not,[34] within the *OC* itself it has an obvious point, suggesting an affinity between the deme and its city so deep and lasting as to blur their distinction.

This applies even when the poet describes Colonus' topography in the most detailed terms. Just as a choral *stasimon* refers both to and beyond its dramatic context, so the poet's topography blends the known and unknown to create a series of references which inevitably draw the audience beyond the specific instance to the general truth it illustrates. The stranger's initial reference to Colonus as the 'brazen-foot threshold, / the stay of Athens' (57-8) seems to be resumed later, in the messenger's speech, and his description of the place at which Oedipus prepares for his death (1590-7):

> And when he came to the *sheer threshold*,
> rooted from the earth with *brazen steps*,
> he stood on one of the many branching paths,
> near the hollow basin, where the pledges
> of Theseus and Peirithous lie, always faithful.
> From there, standing midway between the Thorician rock
> and the hollow pair-tree and on the marble tomb
> he took his seat; then he loosed his filthy clothes.

This 'sheer threshold ... with brazen steps' may be interpreted as a local feature known to the audience, but unclear to us (so Jebb);[35] an allusion to the threshold in the shrine of the Eumenides on the Areopagus;[36] a reference to an entry into Hades known at Eleusis, resuming other references to mystery cult,[37] and perhaps figured here for Colonus itself (the scholia to 1590 and 1595 claim that the 'sheer threshold' was the site of Persephone's disappearance, and the 'Thorician rock' as 'known to the locals'); or as a liminal space between Athenian territory and the wild; the turning point of Oedipus' life; and so on.[38] This polyvalence need not exclude any alternatives, for it makes the link with Athens and reinforces the current story's numinous and legendary qualities, connecting it with Eleusinian mystery cult and other places beyond Colonus (Chapter 5, pp. 81-3).[39]

Moving backwards and forwards in myth and space is an essential part of the topography in this speech: 'on one of the many branching paths' (*keleuthôn en poluskhistôn miâi* 1592) similarly suggests Oedipus' fateful encounter with Laius at the 'split path' between Delphi, Daulis and Phocis (*skhistê hodos OT* 733), while the pledges of Theseus and Peirithous recall another (unsuccessful) trip into the underworld,[40] and the Thorician rock Demeter's own passage into Attica and her gift

101

of the Eleusinian mysteries.[41] Whether the audience is meant
to believe that these features are or once were part of Colonan
topography, they connect the *OC* with many other stories and
themes in heroic legend, against which background the audience's experience is all the more informed.[42]

This fits nicely with Sophocles' mythological procedure
(Chapter 3, pp. 39-45), suggesting a flexible and meaningful
relationship between the worlds of the play and its audience. In
several ways, Colonus is both a real place distinct from Athens,
and an imagined *topos* inextricably linked with its 'mother city'
and the totality of Attica. The city-hinterland dynamic was of
course extremely important, and in Athens' case that territory
was divided into demes which were not merely urban constituents, but communities with their own cultic, political,
economical and cultural identities.[43] Indeed, Cleisthenes' reforms in the late sixth century were central to the basis of
Athenian democracy, in that his deme-divisions cut across familial ties to create a true community of interests.[44] Deme
membership became the predicate of citizenship, and hence-
forth a man was known by reference to it (as well as his father),
as 'Sophocles of Colonus' on the tribute list (T 18).[45]

However, the dynamic came under tremendous strain during
the Peloponnesian War, for Athens had turned almost into an
island, looking largely towards the navy for its provisioning.
The Spartan fortification of Decelea (413 BC) had made some
parts of the countryside unsafe for long stretches of time,
though its effects have been exaggerated. Against the common
notion that the Athenians did not venture out beyond their
walls, or that their countryside was defenceless and utterly
ravaged during this period,[46] there is good evidence that some
demes were not even evacuated, while the Peloponnesians were
never able effectively to threaten the Athenian plain itself,
which was protected by the cavalry:[47] as we saw in Chapter 1,
there were at least two such encounters in the vicinity of
Colonus in the very recent past (410 and 407 BC). Furthermore,
daily cavalry excursions were sent to keep the Peloponnesians
bottled up in Decelea, Colonus' environs were sufficiently secure to host the assembly in 411 BC (though cult equipment was
removed to Athens),[48] forts in the hinterland continued to be
garrisoned, and Athenian patrols were sent even into the far
countryside.

6. Athens and Attica

So the stranger's description of Colonus as the 'stay of Athens' (58) is not nostalgia, but a reflection of its contemporary role in Athens' defence, at least before Sophocles' death in 406 BC: protected by cavalry, scene of victorious encounters, and (with its Poseidon cult) prominent in the self-fashioning of the Athenian *hippeis*. If the portrait is no fantasy, neither is its optimism for the future. Eveline Krummen has recently related the play (and several others) to increased fortification of these sites by the Athenians during the Peloponnesian War within a 'policy of cult-places', by which they were developed and protected 'as a means of controlling the country, but also as a sort of religious fortification, meant to ensure both the protection of the gods and heroes, and on the other hand, to keep the enemy off.'[49] The *OC* is not an historical commentary: instead, background helps to contextualise, to relate the recent to the heroic past and its democratic future.

This remains true even in the aftermath of the Peloponnesian War. Viewed narrowly, Colonus' role counteracts the aristocratic tone of Poseidon *Hippios*, and the association between the oligarchic revolution of 411 BC and the Thirty Tyrants in 404-403 BC. As the *OC*'s *locus* of proven Athenian resistance to historical as well as heroic Peloponnesian aggression, its apologetic effect is also served when aristocratic cavalry and democratic navy are joined through the pairing of Athene and Poseidon in the first *stasimon* (and elsewhere). What is true of the divinities' support and immanence in Colonus is also true of Athens, and their linking reaffirms the things which made Athens great, and which ensure the longer-term survival of a political unit which had only just agreed, through the issuing of an amnesty (autumn 403 BC), to begin its own healing process.

Just as the deme is not merely a cipher for the city, so there are individual elements to the poet's presentation of Athens. Aside from the blurring strategy discussed above, whereby the virtues of Colonus are transferred to, and shared with, those of the urban centre, the image of Athens in the *OC* is in many respects a traditional one, firstly in its pious support of suppliants (see Chapter 5, p. 76),[50] which Oedipus calls to his aid (258-62, 282-3; cf. also 24-5, 106-8). Though his descriptions have an obvious rhetorical purpose, their opinion about Athenians is assumed also by Theseus (913-14):

> ... a city which makes a practice of justice
> and has no power that is without *nomos*.

As already remarked (Chapter 4, p. 55), *nomos* is a very important word, usually translated as 'law' (written or unwritten), but meaning anything from 'custom' to 'proper behaviour', particularly when compared to the dictates of 'nature' (*physis*) – a common (though not always necessary) polarity at this period. Here it is linked with the procedure through which Creon should have fulfilled his mission (924f.), opposed to the violence he used instead (916, 922). Indeed, Theseus' following explanation of the right course reveals an important theme to Athens' depiction – Theseus himself.

Any discussion of Athenian virtues is incomplete without Theseus, whose character is examined in the next chapter; here note only his moderation and caution in every task, particularly when considering the operation of the divine, but also the swiftness and determination he exhibits at the play's crucial moments, firstly when summoned against Creon and then responding to the thunderclaps at the play's end (Chapter 7, pp. 110-16). More than anyone else he is Athens' authority and prestige, and so the way in which other Athenians defer to him is an important element in the depiction of an harmonious community. Particularly revealing in this connection is his summoning of aid, sending someone to stir (898-900)

> the whole people,
> unhorsed and horsed from the sacrifice
> to hasten with unchecked reins

and his assurance that, should the Thebans escape this band, 'there are others to pursue them' (1023). The chorus follow up this picture of unity by terming the pursuing band 'those who belong to Theseus' (*Thêseidân* 1066), using a patronymic epithet (resonant of epic, where it shows familial relationship). Unified behind Theseus, an epic hero re-imagined in Athenian form, the citizens of Athens and Colonus present a formidable, united front against Theban aggression, and a considerable contrast to the picture of that city's *stasis*.

How does this relate to the reality confronting the audience and the poet? Modern accounts tend to speak of a strong dis-

104

junction between Sophocles' ideal and the uncomfortable circumstances in the first half of the Decelean War. Athens was now the 'tyrant city' (according to Thucydides),[51] in charge of an empire which no longer wanted her 'protection' and openly resented her control. However, as outlined in Chapter 1, an expectation of total defeat was not the only one to be entertained in this period. After Sicily, and indeed after the revolution, Athens had recovered and campaigned aggressively – and with some notable successes – in the Ionian theatre, and seemed to be holding her own in the Attic hinterland.

Perhaps more importantly, the *post eventum* clarity so characteristic in modern treatments of Athenian history during this period is rarely afforded the participants. Thus, for instance, Gordon Kirkwood pointed out the contrast between the *OC*'s just Athens which protects the weak against the strong, and the imperial Athens which, e.g., reduced the relatively innocuous island of Melos to destruction and slavery in 416-415 BC.[52] But the treatment of Melos was hardly 'anything strikingly new in the military conduct of Athens *or in the contemporary practice of warfare*',[53] while Sophocles had served as general at the height of Athens' imperial expansion and consolidation, indeed during the ruthless suppression of the Samian revolt (441-439 BC).[54] At the same time, the Athens of the *OC* does not act without an eye on practicalities and its own advantage (Chapter 5, pp. 76-9): Oedipus is made an Athenian citizen principally on the basis of his future benefit, a benefit directed specifically against Thebes and seemingly ensured by Delphi. Theseus' outrage at Creon's behaviour is caused by what he feels is the slight to *his* honour as well as that of his city (902-3, 911, 917-18),[55] reinforcing the chorus' earlier reaction in the same vein (841-3, 879). The King even implies that Creon's desire to return Oedipus to Theban territory is no terrible thing; the crucial factor is that Theseus would have acted differently (924-8):

> Truly I would never have entered your land,
> not even if I had the most just pretext,
> without the consent of the land's ruler, whoever he was,
> neither would I have dragged off nor led away, but I would have known
> how it is necessary for a *xenos* to behave in the presence of townsmen.

105

Piety was not without its calculations, and not every suppliant had to be honoured (Chapter 5, p. 76). Once refuge was granted, of course, it became a matter of pride and self-belief, as well as a desire to avoid divine wrath, which demanded their energetic protection.[56]

Perhaps, therefore, as with the image of Colonus itself, we have become accustomed to seeing the play's issues with too modern (dare I say 'post-colonial'?) a set of presuppositions about the nature of empire, and a view of Athenian prospects which has the benefit of hindsight. The Athenians themselves were more pragmatic than many of the classical tradition's guardians in our own time, which helps to explain the tenacity with which they held on to their empire, but also the images of themselves which had helped to earn and maintain it: 'it is hard to believe that Sophocles was really writing Athens' death lament in 406'.[57] The gods' support, immanent in the very earth and territory of Athens, founded on the harmony between deme and city, is bolstered by the saving presence of the wrathful Theban hero Oedipus, whose protection extends over and guarantees the city' past, present and future. As the chorus say at the approach of Creon and his retinue (726-7):

> Even if I am old,
> the strength of this land has not grown old.

Faced with the threat of a powerful enemy, they reassure Oedipus and the audience in the theatre of Dionysus that, enemies, invasions and setbacks – even defeat – notwithstanding, the greatness of Athens endures. If one were to attempt a sentence length summary of the play, or rather Sophocles' view of Athens, this is it.

7

Characters

Though character is a controversial topic in Greek tragedy,[1] Sophocles' biographical tradition thought it an important part of his art: the *Life* (T 1.21) claims that he 'knows how to draw together his matters so as to construct an entire character from a small half line or one phrase; and this is the greatest thing in poetry, to show character or feeling', while according to Plutarch (T 100) Sophocles praised his own 'mature' style, 'which was the most expressive of character and the best'. Dominated by Oedipus, the *OC* has a particularly rich supporting cast, with whom we begin.

1. Antigone and Ismene

Oedipus' daughters, in complete contrast to their brothers, support their father to their own disadvantage. This is perhaps more evident in Antigone's case, for she accompanies him in exile (345-52, 744-52 1254-64), while Ismene brings him news from Thebes and has – aside from a brief appearance in the *exodos* – the dramatic functions of reporting the latest oracle and fulfilling off stage the rite to the Eumenides (503-9), where she is captured by Creon's men. Though she reappears later on, the three-actor rule (Chapter 2, n. 10) means that she is allotted no more speech until the final lamentation and exchange with Antigone, who still manages to take the prominent role (1670-1750 & ff.).

It is no surprise, then, that she is much more fully drawn as a character. Beyond being a helper, Antigone is given the tasks of persuading the chorus to allow her father to stay (237-53), and her father to hear Polyneices (1181-1203). Motivated by a profound love and sense of familial duty which Oedipus powerfully contrasts with his sons' appalling behaviour (1365-9), she sees for them both, as he tells the stranger (33-4), an ability

107

revealed when she informs him of the stranger's entrance and exit (29f., 82-3), guides him step by step from the grove (173ff.), and announces the entrances of Ismene (310-23), Creon (720-1, 722-3) and Polyneices (1249-51). It is one of the play's heaviest ironies that, in the final scene, he is now the one guiding the group which includes Theseus and his two daughters, and her importance and influence in these terms recedes as Oedipus' power and status grows. Indeed, it is now she at the end who is asking for guidance (1459, 1474, 1488), making a strong contrast with their first interactions, which were marked by a string of questions from an uncertain old man about the location (1-2, 3-6, 23, 30 etc.) and their course of action (170 etc.).[2] But there is more to her character, for she has a sense of moderation (at least in these early scenes) signally lacking in Oedipus. For instance, she persuades him to come out of the grove at the entreaty of the chorus, since 'we must heed things equally as the townsmen, yielding what we must even if unwilling' (171-2). After the chorus recoil from Oedipus, and seem inclined to go back on their original promise of allowing him to remain in his resting place (176 and 226), Antigone asks for their pity – if not for her father, at least for her situation (237-54), and her appeal is intensified by being sung (formally part of the *parodos*). Though Oedipus persuades the chorus to fetch their ruler to decide on his supplication, her duty and compassion make a powerful, positive impression (254-7).

This initial portrait gives Antigone tremendous authority, which she turns successfully towards convincing Oedipus to receive his son (1181-1203). Moreover, after his initial speech seems to to be running out of steam, she encourages Polyneices to use all the rhetorical skill at his disposal (1280-3), but in her earlier speech she makes a remarkable argument (1185-1203):

Be sure, words not spoken to your advantage
will not drag you by force from your opinion.
But what harm is it to listen to his words? Things found
ill are proven so by speech.
You bore him; so that, not even if he does ill to you
in the most impious of terrible evils, my father,
is it right for you to pay him back in ill wise.
Have compassion for him. Others too have bad children
and a sharp temper, but when they are advised
their natures are charmed by the spells of their loved ones.

7. Characters

And you, look to those things, not the present ones,
but the paternal and maternal pains you endured,
and if you see them, I know, you will know how ill a result
accrues from an ill temper.
For you have no small matters of rumination,
deprived of your unseeing eyes.
But yield to us. For it is not good when
those needing justice have to persist, nor that when you
have experienced well (i.e. from us), you know not how to pay
back that experience.

For Antigone, the link between parent and child is so sacred –
a striking point to make to an incestuous parricide – that
nothing could justify revenge:[3] earlier she said that 'everything
is dear (*philon*) to a parent' (1108), and in her initial plea to the
chorus she began her list of things assumed as *philon* to them
with children (250-1). Though in the later scene she only uses
the term when speaking of good men being persuaded by their
philoi (1193-4), it is clear what her concept of *philia* is. It is
shared with her sister: when Ismene leaves the stage to perform
the rites of the Eumenides, she says that 'in the case of parents,
not even if someone should toil, must there be notice of that toil'
(508-9). This is, of course, entirely alien to Oedipus. Antigone
implores him to learn from his experiences (as he had claimed
7-8), and not to cause for his son the suffering he had endured,
and deplored in his first apology (271-4). Present during that
earlier scene, Antigone draws on a theme which Oedipus had
used there as self-exculpation, but she does so in order to break
the cycle of destruction within the household, not to justify it.
Moreover, she is all too aware of his 'sharp spirit' (1193), and
imputes at least some role to that in the 'paternal and maternal
pains' (1196) which Oedipus has already suffered (as Creon had
also noted; above, pp. 117-18). Her speech illuminates several
important things about this exiled duo.

Though she could not do so by persuasion,[4] Antigone also
unites her father and brother in affection. Sophocles brings this
out in two linked scenes, the reunion effected by Theseus (1099-
1118), and Antigone's attempt to prevent Polyneices rejoining
the Argive army (1413-46): in both cases the female, who happens to be the sister of the male she's addressing, attempts to
persuade them to act against their desires and save their
family. Neither can do so, though Oedipus agrees at least to

109

listen to Polyneices. In both cases, the themes of familial love and its loss play a prominent role, and they make clear the fragility of Antigone's fate, tossed between the rivalries and personalities of her household's male members. It may be true, as Polyneices says, that she is 'unworthy in the eyes of all to meet with ill fortune' (1446), but they place her in exactly that situation.

Yet Antigone is not simply a monochromatically 'good' woman. Her final appearance, in the *kommos* separating the *exodos*' two halves, begins to show an intertext with the *Antigone* (Chapter 3, pp. 49-50), as her own persistence (or intransigence) emerges in the exchanges with Ismene and Theseus. First, the sisters return lamenting for their father (a traditional female function), focusing in typical fashion on their future difficulties without father[5] or community (1670-1719). Then Antigone desires to return to her father's tomb, impatient with Ismene's queries about the rectitude of doing so (1730-1), before wanting to die there (1733). She then repeats to Theseus her wish to see the tomb (1756-7) and, when it is denied, demands explanation from him (1759). Reminiscent of her father's similarly stubborn doubts about Theseus' protection (below, pp. 112-13), her resistence comes despite being told by Oedipus that only Theseus was to know his tomb's location (1640-4). Though she has hitherto seemed almost unrelated to Oedipus, the poet hints, as she returns to Thebes (Chapter 2, p. 34 and n. 13), that Antigone does indeed have his blood.

2. Theseus

Theseus has by far the easiest time in this play.[6] Authoritative and kind, he provides a powerful contrast with the three Theban rulers – two past, one hopeful – with whom he comes into contact. We first hear of him in the conversation between Oedipus and the stranger (66-71):

> **Oed**. Does someone rule them, or is discussion the province of the crowd?
> **Str**. Rule is held by the king in the city.
> **Oed**. This man, who is he who rules with reason and might?
> **Str**. Theseus is he called, the child of the former king Aegeus.[7]
> **Oed**. Could someone go to him as envoy from you?
> **Str**. To say what, or to prepare his coming?

The passage sets Theseus' authority and importance alongside the very epic qualities of 'reason and might'. Like his Theban counterparts, Theseus must exist across the distance between the aristocratic / monarchic world of epic and Athens' democratic present, but he manages it much better than they. His determinative role is set well before he appears: though the stranger summons initially authoritative (226) locals to decide Oedipus' fate (77-80), he also fetches Theseus (297-8), to whom the chorus are happy to leave the final decision (294-5), and whose concern for the city (in their eyes) guarantees his personal attention (296-308). Oedipus insists on that before he reveals the nature of his benefit (288-91), and he will do so once more at the play's end, after recognising the thunderclaps as the signs of his impending doom (1457-61, 1472-6, 1486-90). Oedipus' anxiety that Theseus should arrive on time emphasises the fact that, although the benefit's effect is intended for the entire community, its form is to be guarded by Theseus alone, and passed on from ruler to ruler (1518-35).[8]

Theseus' concern for his community is apparent on his arrival (551f.), for his first question is about Oedipus' appeal to the city and himself. He does not ask for the 'great benefit', but spends most of this first speech stressing his own pity (555-6, 565-6) and a shared experience of exile, which manages to enhance Theseus' stature (esp. 563-4) as much as it establishes sympathy. Though there is calculated caution to his words, his closing *gnômê* ('since / I know that I am a man and that I have / no greater share in the morrow than you' 566-8) reveals a moderation, and a perspective on shared humanity, not usually found in a tragic autocrat. Pity and self-interest need not be mutually exclusive, as Oedipus notes ('what worthy man is not a friend to himself?' 309), and Theseus questions him closely about the precise nature and timing of the boon (579-81). He can't quite believe that Oedipus will require only burial (583-4, 586) and, on being warned that the decision is no light one (587), swiftly uncovers the ramifications of his pity. Theseus is, in short, a pragmatic *and* restrained ruler: he advises Oedipus that his anger against the Thebans is unwise (592), stressing once again the importance of 'practicality' (*xumphoron* 592), but he also recognises that he should not judge Oedipus' anger 'without full understanding' (594). Moreover, he is not gullible, finding it hard to believe Oedipus'

111

assertion he could ever have cause for enmity with Thebes (606).

The equality between them is clear *inter al.* from that the fact that only they are described (repeatedly) as 'noble' (*gennaios*): Oedipus first invokes his nobility (*to gennaion*) as that which has taught him contentment (8), and the stranger remarks on his *gennaion* appearance (76), while (in the messenger's speech) the old man tells his daughters they have to endure *to gennaion* (1640, marked doubtful in the OCT). The messenger deployed the same word a few lines earlier (1636) to denote Theseus' guardianship over Ismene and Antigone, as indeed did Oedipus himself when complimenting Theseus' opening speech (569), and when wishing that his own nobility should benefit them (as Theseus departs to rescue the daughters 1042-3).[9]

Concomitantly, Theseus is an heroic figure in his own right: he responds in a somewhat nettled manner when Oedipus doubts the firmness of his pledge (648-67), even breaking into his sentences (652-6 & ff.) before reassuring him that 'even if I am not here, I know that my name will guard you from suffering ill' (666-7). Honour and authority are as much an issue as for any other hero, and he doesn't enjoy having them questioned. Our first impression of Theseus is, therefore, of a hero mindful of his prerogatives and a king protective of his community, yet for all that also an intelligent man with an understanding of suffering and the limitations of humankind. His motives for accepting Oedipus into the city enshrine these characteristics, and all of them – honour and authority, moderation and pragmatism – will be tested and proven in the play's course.

The first of these – honour – is important for all tragic autocrats, for whom the personal is generally inextricable from the political. Theseus feels infringements here no less than any other character, barking his outrage at Creon (902-3; 911-12; 917-18):

> … so that the maids do not go past, *and I become a source of laughter*
> to/by this stranger here, worsted by his violence.

> since you have acted neither *worthily of me*
> nor those from whom you are sprung nor your land

and you thought that *my city* was empty of men or
some slave-city, *and that I was worth nothing.*

All these charges are felt equally as a slight upon Athens, yet
there are also hints of a potential overbalance in that relationship (1028-33):

> well do I know that you (sc. Creon)
> have come neither unarmed nor unprepared
> to such an extent of violence in your current daring,
> but there is someone trusting in whom you did this.
> I must watch for this, nor make this city
> weaker than one man.

Theseus seems to be referring at first to Creon's attendants, and
the need for someone of his martial ability to combat such a
group. Yet 1031 refers to someone inside Athens. However
typically Greek it is 'to explain disaster by treason',[10] one is
reminded of Oedipus himself in the *OT*, who treats Laius'
murder out of self-interest (*OT* 137-40, 252-68) and assumes
treacherous activity in Thebes itself (*OT* 124-5), which he then
sees in both Creon and Teiresias. In Theseus' mouth, for all his
positive characteristics, it summons the paranoia of the tragic
autocrat, swift to see sedition everywhere.[11] Indeed, we have
already seen a certain tetchiness in this regard (648-67 above),
and we see it again when Oedipus finally agrees to hear Polyneices' suit (1206-10):

> **Oed**. Only, my host, if that man comes here thus,
> let no one ever have power over my life.
> **Th.** Once is enough for such words, I do not wish to hear them
> twice,
> old man. And I do not wish to boast; know that you
> are safe, if, that is, one of the gods protects me too.

Theseus knows that his decision and his honour are tightly
bound together: to question one is to question the other, and
while here it may express Oedipus' faults more than Theseus' –
particularly after he has just won an encounter to prove his
pledge – the autocrat's self-control is best not put to the test.
Theseus shows more of it than anyone else in this play, alongside an ever present sense of humanity and moderation.

This is shown by his regard for the divine, e.g. in attending the sacrifice to Poseidon, from which he is called twice – by Oedipus and the chorus after Creon's theft of his daughters (887-90), and then after the thunderbolts alert Oedipus to the immediacy of his fate (1500-4).[12] Aside from his inference that the gods do wish Oedipus to have a home in Athens (634), Theseus persuades Oedipus to listen to his son because of the suppliant posture he has taken (1179-80), picking up one of his own reasons for accepting Oedipus into Athens (634-5) and so turning his guest's success to good persuasive use. He also refuses to allow Antigone and Ismene to continue weeping at the end of the play on the grounds that it would darken the *kharis* ('favour') of the underworld powers (1751-3),[13] and he immediately respects Oedipus' wish about the secrecy of his grave by denying Antigone's repeated requests to see it (1758, 1760-7). This quality, or perhaps a caution deriving from it, is also clear in his silence when Oedipus mentions his own *miasma* as the reason for him not to take and kiss Theseus' hand (1132-6).[14]

The Athenian's reward for this piety is to witness Oedipus' final moment, the vision of divinity which accompanies it (1648-56), and to have earned for his community Oedipus' preternatural aid. Just as with the question of his authority, however, there is also a subtle reminder of Theseus' shortcomings in his observances, in the messenger's description of the place where Oedipus meets his doom (1593-4) 'near the hollow rock, where the pledges / of Theseus and Peirithous lie, faithful always'. As a symbol of Theseus' failed co-attempt to rape Persephone (from which Heracles rescued Theseus and (in some versions) Peirithous as well), the 'pledges' not only recall the 'pledge of my fate' of which Oedipus speaks (46), but also hint that the Athenian king is not a model of perfection. One might pursue the negative implications further, and suggest that the story refers to the eternal prison in which Peirithous was stuck. It would be somewhat like the oath Theseus gives Oedipus to care for his daughters (1631-5), yet his first action is to allow them to return to Thebes, sworn enemy of Oedipus (1768ff.). This may be too harsh, as Antigone's purpose ('to see if somehow we might prevent the murder coming to our brothers' 1770-2) seemed reasonable enough, and the pledges could represent positively the fidelity of a man bound to go even into Hades.[15] Additionally, as this is the place where

Oedipus disappears, it would create another level in their sympathy of experience.[16]
Theseus counsels moderation and restraint against self-destructive anger, firstly when Oedipus explains his reluctance to return home (592-4 above), but again when Oedipus seems prepared not even to hear Polyneices speak (1175-6):

> What? Can you not listen, and then not do the things
> you don't want? Why is it painful to you to hear this man?

Of course, Theseus can practice his preaching, refusing to boast about his achievements (1143-59; also 1208-10), checking his initial desire to punish Creon personally for his outrages (914-16),[17] as well as to point out what his own strategy would have been, had he been in Creon's shoes – namely, to do nothing without the consent of the land's ruler (924-8) (again revealing the importance of autocratic power). Indeed, in answering Creon's attempt to lay the blame for his actions on the community, Theseus even excuses Thebes of responsibility for Creon's actions (918-23) – a moment of neat political pragmatism, turning the mission of an entire city into a single man's wrongdoing. Nor is this an isolated example of his practicality. He shows despatch in sending men to retrieve Antigone and Ismene (897-901), in planning for the eventuality that they may escape his current efforts (1020-4), and in using Creon as a hostage (932-4, 1016-17). Even in hurrying to Oedipus' final summons, he has already noted the natural clamour and intuits its divine cause (1500-4), before questioning the old man closely about his proofs (1505-18) and submitting to his interpretation of the signs.
Theseus is a ruler worthy of both the benefit and the responsibility of being the guardian of Oedipus' tomb. His character is a particularly fortuitous mixture: powerful and pious, kind and practical, he is the positive image of the tragic autocrat, properly motivated, self-controlled, and driven by his concern for his city. Nonetheless, he also shows the typical traits of the autocrat – touchiness, suspicion – which have led elsewhere to disaster.[18] Though Athens may be 'a city practising justice / and determining nothing without law' (913-14), the poet is quite careful to raise some subtle doubts about its leader. If Theseus has avoided error in this play, he is still a ruler of the type

Oedipus and Creon were, and which Polyneices aspires to be. He indicates to an Athenian audience what that figure, even in the best of possible heroic worlds, could be.

3. Creon

Creon has suffered, deservedly, from a bad press, but he has a difficult job to do.[19] We first meet him when he arrives to persuade Oedipus to return to Thebes, though his behaviour there is already contextualised by Ismene's narrative (367-73):

> For before it pleased them to leave to Creon
> the throne and not to defile the city,
> their reason being the ancient destruction of the family,
> which held firm your wretched house.
> But now from one of the gods and from their sinful minds
> there has come to them, thrice wretched,
> to seize power and the tyrant's rule.

And her description of Creon's intentions (399-400):

> so as to set you near the Theban land, to have control
> over you, but that you not step foot in the borders of that land.

The first passage reminds the audience of the Creon of the *OT*, who (against the paranoia of Oedipus) claimed that he was happy to possess influence without authority and all its attendant responsibility (*OT* 584-602). The second passage renders Creon's first speech obviously false, for he makes no mention of this central qualification. Nor does he bring up the fact, later revealed (818-19), that he had already seized Ismene (who left the stage at 507-9), and that he had armed attendants to do the work. Instead, he begins by seeking to disarm the Athenian chorus (728-34):

> Well born inhabitants of this land,
> I see from your eyes that you have taken new
> fear from my arrival;
> do not fear me nor send an evil word my way.
> For I have come with no plan to do anything, since
> I am an old man, and I know that I come
> to a city, if any in Greece, of mighty strength.

116

At this stage, all appears reasonable. But, with the injunctions that Oedipus should return to the 'plain of the Cadmeians (i.e. Thebans)' (740), 'to his home' (741) and later to the city and 'your paternal home' (757), his duplicity is revealed. His claim to act for the whole community may well be true, but Eteocles is in charge of a hardly democratic, or even proto-democratic, Thebes. Creon also claims that he was chosen because of his familial link with Oedipus (739-40), and tries to appeal to their similarity in age, bewailing thus his circumstance while focusing on the terrible plight of Antigone 'for any passerby to snatch' (752) – this last rather threatening, given what he has done and will try. His plea's basic structure (description of Oedipus' plight followed by self-reproach) is shared with Polyneices' following attempt (cf. below), though Creon winds up with an injunction to speak well of Athens 'for she is worthy; but your own city would be more justly honoured, for she was your nurse of old' (759-60).

Such a reminder of family and community connections serves no purpose with Oedipus, who hurls them back at him: they did not prevent the original exile (765-71), and the 'nurse of old' reminds him that he was thrown out both as a child and again more recently, so that its nursing is hardly a happy theme (see below, pp. 129-31). His anger at Creon's self-presentation is unsurprising, and it leads into a series of clashes in which Creon in his turn becomes more heated at Oedipus' barbs, seizes and removes Antigone and then attempts to do the same to her father (857 & ff.). In this his true nature and mission are revealed. Having begun by complimenting the strength of Athens, he now openly threatens the city (837) and denies its authority to prevent him (883). In the midst of this escalation, Creon accurately describes his kinsman (852-5):

> For at last, I know, you will realise this,
> that you do good to yourself neither now
> nor did you do it in the past, against your *philoi*
> giving into your anger, which always destroys you.

As a description of Oedipus, Creon has hit the nail right on the head (as Antigone will later, 1193f.), but he fails – like all the males of this house – to realise how well it fits him. Indeed, Creon tries to excuse his behaviour before Theseus (939-59), and his apology is in many ways redolent of Oedipus' own: he claims kinship with the fugitives – not any low opinion of Athens – as his first reason, the unwillingness of the Athenians to nurture (*trephein* 943) such a criminal character as Oedipus as his second, and the anger roused in him as his third (951-3). The logical relationship between these is problematic: the first two depict the seizure as his purpose before he arrived, the third frames it as a rage-induced accident. Furthermore, the seizures (818-47, 860f.) took place before Oedipus' curse (868-70), not *because* of it, as he claims.[20] Finally, Creon's failure to mention to Theseus the real reason behind his mission, as well as his earlier seizure of Ismene, destroys his defence as a whole.

But Creon is convinced that he has the best interests of his city at heart: he had not contested the throne with Eteocles and Polyneices (though details are not forthcoming), he considers himself sent by all his citizens, he is resolute in the face of Theseus' threats (956-8, 1036-7), and Thebes' fortunes are not simply a question of his individual power. Nonetheless, Creon does not come out well. His unsuccessful efforts are marked by deceit and violence, an impious disregard for the rights of the sheltered suppliant, and a very Oedipal (or Labdacid?) rhetoric – flawed and convinced. As Theseus points out, whatever his claim's justice, Creon should not have offended against his own authority and Athens' sovereignty (924-8). But the audience has also heard a critique of Oedipus' behaviour from someone with long experience, and who seems to act similarly, viz. beginning from a reasonable position but allowing anger to get the better of him (see below, pp. 121-33). They are thus prepared for the next approach from another would-be Theban ruler, another kinsman of Oedipus.

4. Polyneices

Given the meaning of his name ('much-quarrel'), it is hardly surprising that Polyneices too has had a bad press, cast variously as a madman for failing to call off the attack on Thebes, and a villain who abandoned his father and sister to a terrible existence.[21] The substance of these charges is true, but Polyneices at least admits his faults towards Oedipus and does not attempt to mitigate his past errors, and also shows with his sisters an affection which is remarkably like that shown

118

by his father. Indeed, the similarities between these two are striking.[22]

Before he enters, we have already met him in Ismene's report (365-83): Polyneices and Eteocles had originally decided to leave the throne to Creon, keeping in mind the ancient doom of Oedipus' family; the idyll was now firmly over, for Eteocles had claimed the throne and exiled his elder[23] brother (though the details are left to his appearance later in the play). This also prepares for the themes of political power throughout the father / son encounter, for Sophocles repeats words based on the stem 'power-' (*krat-*) throughout Ismene's report and Oedipus' reply (392, 400, 405, 408), and his following curse (421ff.) is dominated by Oedipus' (somewhat partial) condemnation of his sons for their political ambition.[24]

Further preparation comes once Oedipus realises the identity of the suppliant at Poseidon's altar (1169). The difficulty with which Theseus and Antigone persuade him even to listen to his son's entreaties does not bode well for Polyneices' attempt, and their success is hardly propitious, given his grudging tone (1204-7):

> Child, heavy is the pleasure you have won from me
> by your speech; so let it be how you wish.
> Only, my host, if that man comes here thus,
> let no one ever gain control of my life.

Polyneices' suppliancy (emphasised before they meet; cf. 1158, 1160, 1163, 1166, 1179)[25] is of course significant, for it places him in somewhat the same position with regard to Oedipus as his father vis-à-vis Theseus (Chapter 5, pp. 78-9), so we compare him not only with Creon but also his father. Of course, Polyneices' own neglect of duty did have something to do with their terrible situation (1254-63), but he launches into a vehement self-reproach unthinkable in Oedipus (1264-70):

> These things, wretch I am, I learn fully far too late.
> And I witness that as the worst of men in your support[26]
> have I come; learn my faults not from others.
> But, since Shame shares the throne with Zeus
> in all deeds, let her stand on your side too,
> father. For of the errors
> there can be a cure, but no addition further.

This compares with Creon, who had expressed regret (744-52) followed by self-reproach (753-5), but the differences are at least as notable:[27] Polyneices comes alone, not thronged with men prepared to do violence (as Antigone notes: 723, 1250-1). Secondly, he comes from the altar of Poseidon in Athenian territory, and so enters the acting area from the audience's right – the opposite side of Creon's entrance and exit. The dramaturgical contrast underlines the poet's not unsympathetic portrait. Of course, Polyneices wants Oedipus' aid, and his opening claim (1264) seems specious. Nonetheless, and unlike his uncle, he does not try to hide his real intention, but lays the situation out fully, mentioning the oracle which Creon had been so careful to hide (1331-2) and so revealing why he has approached his father, as well as his hopes for throwing out Eteocles. However, his narrative of the fraternal quarrel is interesting, and paints a more coloured picture of his motivation (1292-8):

> I am driven from my paternal land an exile,
> since I thought it right to sit in full
> power on your throne because I am the elder in birth.
> For which Eteocles, though younger born,
> pushed me from the land, not by conquering me in debate
> nor coming to a trial of hands nor deeds,
> but by persuading the city.

By virtue of precedence, and spurning the idea that the community could have a role in choosing its leader, Polyneices seeks the monarchic, autocratic ideal, and fails to explain the overthrow of the original circumstance (from Ismene's speech). His narrative makes him the instigator of the trouble, and places Eteocles in the relatively more favourable situation (at least in the eyes of an Athenian audience) of ruling with his people's consent.[28] To a wannabe autocrat, this is simply beyond the pale, but it allows him to try (as Theseus 562-8)[29] to level his experience with Oedipus' as exiles (1334-7) and the objects of Eteocles' mockery (1338-9), before admitting that 'without you, I have not even the strength to survive' (1344-5).

These links notwithstanding, Oedipus' rejection, (renewed?)[30] curses and prediction of failure make it clear to Polyneices that he will fail, thus placing great emphasis on the following exchange with Antigone (1399-1446). Its essence is her attempt to dissuade him from the attack, but its reveals his motivations and character. Polyneices resists her pleas, for he cannot bear the thought of 'being laughed at' (as Theseus, 902-3; above, pp. 112-13), particularly given his position as the elder, for 'flight is shameful' (1422). He would never be able to resummon a host for the same purpose (1418-19) if he were to retreat now, and he will even conceal the news from the army on the rather reasonable basis (at least, in other circumstances) that a good leader does not undermine his troops' morale (1429-30). He understands that death is necessary under the circumstances constructed by his father and his 'Erinyes' (see Chapter 5, pp. 71-4), before which he shows a resigned dignity. Aside from this, the exchange reveals deep sibling affection. Antigone, utterly unlike Oedipus, shows no anger towards him for his role in their sufferings, and exhibits real grief at the thought of his death (1427, 1439-40, 1442-3).

Though only briefly on display, Polyneices exhibits an admirable resolve before death, coupled with an awareness of his faults and a desire to fix them. He is, nonetheless, determined to bring an army to ruin in his own service and for his own ends, overturning his fatherland in the process, and fixated upon sole power as the only reliable index of his honour.[31] In his inability to apply to others principles he claims for himself, in his single-minded refusal to bend, as well as in the love for his sister and determination to destroy his brother, Polyneices is very much his father's son.

5. Oedipus

The progression in Oedipus' fortunes dominates the course of the *OC*, its focal moment his reception into Athens. Before he was the suppliant seeking support; now he is a desirable possession. Though seemingly weak, Oedipus bears tremendous power and the character to go with it, for he is practically immovable, remaining in the general area of the Eumenides' grove throughout the play.[32] The *prologos* sets the pattern of people approaching Oedipus, so his success does not radically change the play's dramatic and dramaturgic direction, which striking continuity suggests others.

The most fundamental consists in the fact that Oedipus is defined constantly by polar contradictions: power and impotence, hatred and love, self-loathing and unshakeable self-be-lief.[33] Related to his increasing proximity to the (fearsome and beneficent) Eumenides and the approach of his hero cult (Chapter 5, pp. 71-4, 79-85), the interaction of these qualities is perfectly exhibited at his first appearance: a pitiful figure whose degradation and resignation contrast vividly with the *OT*'s all powerful ruler. He stumbles onto the stage, guided only by his daughter, defining himself by his blindness as soon as he speaks (1), a wanderer in need of the small gift of protection (3-5), with small needs and desires (5-6), and worldview to match (7-8). His readiness to 'complete whatever we hear' (i.e. 'are told') (13) reveals a passivity reflected also in his dependence on Antigone (19-35). Aside from his need for an Athenian reception, Oedipus' physical dependence is a constant theme: Antigone guides him out of the grove (155-69), and his progress is slow and painful (170-202); arriving characters' identities need to be announced (e.g. 310-23); after his protestations of weakness (495-502), Ismene has to perform the rite to the Eumenides, leaving Antigone with an instruction to guard their father (503-9); he cannot prevent the seizure of his daughters without the chorus' (unsuccessful) aid (813-86), and would have been similarly unable in his own case were it not for Theseus (887f.).

Yet, as he had tried to influence his fate despite losing power in the *OT*, Oedipus seeks to exercise control[34] from the play's start, where he refuses to leave the grove (44-6):[35]

> **Oed**. But may (the Eumenides) receive their suppliant with favour;
> since never hereafter would I leave this seat.
> **Str**. What is this? **Oed**. The watchword of my fortune.

The victory of his latent power over his patent impotence is traced in the 'teaching' (*didaskein*) theme: Oedipus claims to have been taught contentment with his lot (7-8), and to be ready to learn from others what he must do. Similarly, he asks the chorus to be taught (468, 480) the rite. His insistent questioning (468, 471, 474, 476, 478, 480, 482) recalls the way he interrogated the stranger (38, 41, 52, 64, 66, 68, 70) and then Ismene (385-6, 388, 391, 393, 398, 401, 406, 410, 412, 414, 416, 418-19), but it does not speak of passivity. For Oedipus, instruction is an

interactive process in which he takes the lead, as when asking
(969) Creon, rhetorically, to teach him how he was wrong to
defend himself against Laius' attack. Though Theseus requests
instruction from Oedipus (560, 575, 594), he eventually has to
stop him (654). When Oedipus asks Theseus to explain his
cryptic words in these terms (1154), it prepares for the reversal in the verb's final two deployments, as Oedipus declares
his readiness to teach Theseus the observance of his tomb
(1518) and then closes a general admonition to respect the
gods with the flattering 'I teach you what you already know'
(1539). The reversal between the first rite to the Eumenides,
where Oedipus requested instruction, to his own last rite,
where he gives it, is the most blatant symbol of his transformation, but his control over the teaching theme is obvious
throughout.

Similarly expressive is the 'small word' (*smîkros logos*)
theme,[36] deployed by Oedipus alone[37] on three occasions: to
refer to the speech his sons failed to give on his behalf when
he was exiled (443); to refer to Theseus' initial welcome in
these terms (569-70); and to denote the trivial pretext which
will overturn any alliance with Thebes (620). On the first two
occasions, it is a desirable thing, on the third negative, a
mere pretext bearing no adequate relationship to its consequences. Just as Oedipus' notion of teaching warped around
his own needs and desires, so he uses the 'small word' in
whatever sense *he* chooses: words will mean what and when
he wants them to. Thematics like this show a constant desire
to dominate even when he has no power, so when Oedipus
closes his prayer to the Eumenides with the claim that he 'is
not the person of old' (110), we may doubt his accuracy to the
same extent that we question the sincerity of his worry, a
little earlier in the same prayer, that he may be beneath the
dread goddesses' notice (104-5). As one 'always / slaving
under the furthest toils of mortals' (105), Oedipus is ever
convinced of his extremity.

This makes it difficult for him to leave matters to others,
twice offending Theseus, first when he presses the Athenian
king about his commitment immediately after his initial promise (650-57):

Oed. Note that I do not bind you with an oath as though you
were a base man.
Th. Indeed, you would not achieve anything further than with my
promise.
Oed. So how will you act? **Th**. Of what are you particularly
afraid?
Oed. Men will come – **Th**. But that will be the concern of these
men here.
Oed. See that you're leaving me – **Th**. Don't teach[38] me the
things I must do.
Oed. A fearful man necessarily – **Th**. My heart knows no fear.
Oed. Do you not know the threats – **Th**. I know that no man will
lead
you from here by force against my will …

He does it again when he grudgingly agrees to listen to Polyneices (1204-10):

Oed. Child, heavy is the pleasure you have won from me
by your speech; so let it be how you wish.
Only, my host, if that man comes here thus,
let no one ever gain control of my life.
Th. Once (is enough for) such things, I do not wish to hear it
twice,
old man. And I do not like to boast. But know
that you are safe, if indeed one of the gods will save me.

Given that Theseus has just fought in order to restore Oedipus'
daughters, it is churlish to question his commitment, but Oedipus is as ill-equipped to leave power to others as he is utterly
convinced in the rectitude of his own position. This self-belief is
fanned by the extraordinary knowledge about his death with
which he starts the play (88-95):

(Phoebus) said that this would be my rest in a long time,
when I came to the land of my goal, where I should seize
the seat of the Reverend Goddesses[39] and a stranger's welcome,
there I should end my wretched life,
dwelling as a gain to those who received me,
but disaster for those who sent me, who drove me out;
and signs of guarantee of these things would come to me,
either a quake, or some thunderbolt, or the flash of Zeus.

124

From this position, inference and deduction bring him to the right end (see Chapter 5, pp. 65-8), but Oedipus had erred in precisely this regard in the *OT*, and in the *OC* his analysis of his own and others' actions is far from infallible, particularly with regard to the central issues of guilt and responsibility (see Chapter 4). These errors serve to underline his self-conviction, and are the necessary inconsistencies into which absolute self-belief pulls him. For instance, in reassuring Theseus that there will come a time when his current good relations with Thebes will sour, Oedipus speaks famously of the operation of time on the changeability of human fortune and affairs, noting that only the gods are immune from death and old age (607-28):[40] complete reversals are commonplace, both with regard to individuals and cities, so Theseus can be assured that his Theban ties will loosen, at which time Oedipus' corpse will 'drink their warm blood' (622).[41] Though immediately contrasted with the Ode to Colonus' aesthetic of permanence (Chapter 5, pp. 93-6), Oedipus does not or cannot apply the direct lesson to himself, even after his protestations of learning through instruction by 'companion time in its great length' (7). Aside from the fact that this is hardly the Oedipus of this (or any) play, he has not come to be satisfied with his situation, holding it bitterly against Creon, Thebes, and his own sons. However powerful his invocation of time and change, it reminds one of nothing so much as the very similar, and similarly deluded, enunciation of this theme by Ajax in his play (*Ajax* 646-92). In fact, Oedipus' persistent anger is more characteristic of the gods (exempted (607-9) from the 'time changes all' principle). Indeed, though Creon notes that 'there is no other old age for anger, / except death' (954-5), the *post mortem* continuity of his anger is an essential part of his power. Oedipus' principles, once more,[42] apply to everybody but him.

Nor is this his only inconsistency. When Ismene brings him news of civil strife in Thebes, he reacts as though oblivious of Apollo's oracle, and his joy on discovering himself in the Eumenides' grove: 'do you still have hope that the gods will have / some care for me, so that I am at last saved?' (385-6) His reaction to the new oracle is, initially, disbelief (391-5):

Oed. Who could do well by the agency of such a man as I?
Is. They say that power over those men comes to be in you.
Oed. When I am no longer, then I am a man?

Is. For now the gods set you upright, and beforehand they destroyed you.
Oed. It is trivial to set upright an old man, when he fell as a young man.

This is all psychologically very plausible, but his bitter self-pity blinds him to a divine favour of which he had very recently been fully and joyfully aware. The fact of his honouring now is no 'trivial' matter, certainly not as he saw it in the opening scene.

However powerful and erroneous Oedipus' rhetoric, Theseus is persuaded by the nature of this benefit, whatever his finer feelings about suffering (above, pp. 111-12). Oedipus' hero cult is largely a more permanent form of the common 'help friends – harm enemies' ethic which underpins the heroic world.[43] Crucial, therefore, is *Oedipus'* definition of those groups. From one point of view, the most natural claim on *philia* comes from his community and his family. Indeed, Creon consistently assumes the existence of *philia*, recognising that there is a contest between Athens and Thebes on precisely this point (758-60):

(come home) to your paternal house, speaking of this city
in a friendly way (*philôs*); for she is worthy; but that one at home
would more justly be revered, since she is your nurse[44] of old.

Accordingly, he is astonished when Oedipus curses his *philoi* (813-14); he justifies his kidnapping of Ismene and Antigone since they are 'mine' (*emous* 832); and he equates the fatherland and Oedipus' *philoi* as those whom he currently outrages (as in the past: 850, 854-5). In one sense Creon is right, in another wrong (for he is trying to trick a *philos* against his best interests),[45] though he has missed the point: not only is Oedipus' *philia* not of the normal kind, but any previous ties were broken before the play begins, and Oedipus' reception into Athens proves their final sundering. The point is made in Oedipus' reply to Creon, where he suggests that 'kinship was in no wise dear (*philon*) to you then' when he was exiled (771), and he defines *philia* according to willingness, asking rhetorically 'and what joy so great, to love those who are unwilling?' (775). He transfers his loyalties from Thebes to Athens, e.g. when he calls Theseus 'o dearest *philos*' (891).[46]

Rejecting in turn the entreaties of Creon and Polyneices, he

7. Characters

dooms both his city and his family. Given the rather messy nature of *philia* in this household, such a step is perhaps inevitable, yet his own *philia* is far from an unqualified good (see also below, pp. 111-12): though he terms Antigone and Ismene 'dearest' (1108 – to which Antigone replies 'everything is dear to a parent') his curse encompasses them as well (earlier called his 'twin disasters' 530-2). Antigone recognises this burden at the play's end, describing the care for her father ('what was never *philon* was *philon*' 1698), but to enjoy his *philia* as a recipient of cultic benefits is another matter, as he seems to acknowledge in his 'time changes all' speech (cf. 163-4). When he speaks of change between men who are *philoi* (612-13), his coming hero cult exempts his benefit to Athens from this change and, with the chorus commanding Oedipus (184-7) 'stranger, endure in a strange land, / o stranger, to hate whatever the city / has raised as un-*philon* / and to reverence what it has as *philon*', it is another sign of the Athenian community's victory over the Theban family.

This is not only a matter of turning away from old connections, but spurning them as well. In effect, his curses and saving presence in Athens explain a future of conflict, and foreground an enmity which is to serve Athenian interests against those of his own people. One must wonder at the justice of his hatreds towards Thebes, Creon and his sons, for the illogicalities here are rife (Chapter 4, pp. 59-64), and focus inevitably on the extremity and intensity of his anger, and his utter inability to criticise himself, or to see his actions within a wider framework. As in the *OT*, where the situation of the city became less and less important as the play went on, (even more) so in the *OC* he never expresses a word of regret or concern about the fate of Thebes itself: told of *stasis* there by Ismene, he only perks up at news of new oracles concerning *him*, becoming the eager, questioning Oedipus of old (388, 398 etc.), though initially still interspersing his queries with resigned and despairing comments (391, 393, 395).[47] His self-centredness is even clearer when informing Creon of his children's coming failure, in that he stresses they shall not have possession of '*my* land' (789-90).

Moreover, this peculiarly intra-familial violence is something characteristic of Oedipus and his family going back to Laius, and its power is beyond reason. Given his increasing identification with the Eumenides, this is not surprising, for

127

they avenged wrongs within the family (Chapter 5, pp. 71-4), and Oedipus even applies a revenge ethic towards his parents (Chapter 4, p. 54)! But his sons bear the brunt of his rage in the *OC* (335-41, 416-52), as he prays implicitly for their deaths in front of Ismene and Antigone (421-7):

> But may the gods never quench their fixed
> strife, and may it be in my power to determine
> the end of this battle for them,
> on which they now grab hold and raise their spears for;
> so would neither the one who now holds the throne and sceptre
> remain, nor the one who left
> would ever return back again.

However deserved a penalty this may seem for their (undoubted) wrongdoing (and filial neglect was a serious charge in contemporary Athens, but the penalty was loss of citizen rights, not death),[48] the lengthiest and most bitter outpouring of his anger is reserved for Polyneices himself (1348-96).[49] This speech crosses every boundary within the family, all the more noticeably after Antigone's unsuccessful plea for the sanctity of those relationships (above, pp. 108-9). Her novel notion represents what Oedipus might have learned from his sufferings, as he claimed to have done in the opening scene of the play. Instead, what his parents had done to him out of necessity, he chooses to do to his son(s) without need.[50]

This failure to learn is also represented in the general reversal of the suppliant situation, for it is now Oedipus who rejects his son's plea (Chapter 5, pp. 78-9). The terseness of his reply to Antigone's appeal (1204-5) is as disappointing an answer to her eloquence as it is an accurate reflection of his character.[51] Forewarned thus, we have a fair intimation of what is to happen. Beginning with an address to the chorus, in which he denies that he would ever have spoken to this figure were it not for Theseus' intervention, Oedipus first utters a personal history which sits ill with his (and other) previous accounts in blaming Polyneices personally for driving him out (1354-64),[52] before comparing his sons' sense of duty rather unfavourably with his daughters'. Shockingly, he predicts Polyneices' death 'stained with blood' (1373-4) alongside his brother, defining his curses' purpose (1377-9):

7. Characters

So that you think it right to honour those who begat you,
and not remove them from honour, if two such as you were
born of a blind father. For my daughters here did not do thus.

It is impossible not to recall Oedipus' earlier anger at his
parents, particularly when he calls down as witness the 'hateful
paternal darkness of Tartarus' (1389-90). Scholars are divided
on the significance of the adjective 'paternal' (*patrôion* 1390),
but it would be fitting that Oedipus should remind the audience
of his own violence (and its justifications) at the very moment
the same reciprocity destroys his sons.

The flipside of all this familial hatred is the love between
father and daughters, which scholarship generally considers to
his credit.[53] Doubtless there is power to his affection, and one
need not point out that it extends only as far as their support of
him, but certainly we can ponder the future he has ensured for
them (1611-19):

> O children,
> there is no longer a father for you on this day,
> For everything of me is dead, and no longer
> will you have this *ill-toiling care* for me.
> *Harsh* it was, I know, children. But one word
> alone will release all your *troubles*.
> For there is none from whom you have
> love more than from this man, deprived of whom
> for the future you will spend out your lives.

This passage represents the culmination of two important
themes. The first is 'raising' / 'care' / 'nursing' (*trophê*),[54] one of
Oedipus' orienting principles: those who performed this duty for
him are favoured, those who did not are not.[55] That theme had
been foregrounded since Ismene's arrival (324ff.), as she called
the condition of her father and Antigone (and herself) 'o ill-
wretched raisings' (*ô dusathliai trophai* 330), and Oedipus'
lengthy condemnation of his sons for their failures (338, 341,
352), comparing them to the gender-inverted Egyptians, where
the men stay at home and women work (337-45).[56] To complete
the picture, he then moved into detailing the care which both
Antigone and Ismene had shown in his service (345-56). The
reversal does not only extend to the brothers, of course, for
Antigone (345-7)

129

from the time when she left off her youthful
rearing (*trophês*) and gained strength in her body,
always with me, ill-portioned she wanders, ...

She had only time to cease childhood (346) before being thrust
into this 'toiling' (*pon-, mochth-* etc.) for her father. This, the
second theme, is constantly connected with nursing, and under-
scores the difficulties associated with maintaining Oedipus.
He asserts that the sons should toil (335, 342), yet it is the
daughters who toil hard (literally 'overtoil' *huperponeîton*
345). Ismene refers to her toils in searching for her father's
'place of nursing' (*trophên* 362), and then (leaving the stage to
perform the Eumenides' rite) remarks (508-9):

For when someone toils (*ponêi*) for their parents,
they should not be mindful of the toil (*ponou*)

In the same way does Oedipus throw back Polyneices' admission (1265-6) 'I call to witness that I am the worst of men in your
care (*trophais*)', by claiming 'and you made me nursed in (*entro-
phon*) toil' (1362) and 'these are men, not women, for their
toiling with me (*sumponein*); / but you two were born from
another, not me' (1368-9). The culmination of these themes in
the farewell narrated by the messenger (1611-19, above), when
Oedipus acknowledges openly how difficult life has been for his
daughters, places tremendous focus on their compensation,
indeed their futures, and one wonders whether his 'love' (*to
philein*) is an adequate return.[57] This 'one word' (1615) is surely
a reference to the 'small word' theme which was something
Oedipus could use in either positive or negative sense according
to his needs and belief (above, p. 123). His claim of *philia* has
not been tremendously reciprocal or practical, for he has made
no arrangement for their futures. Certainly by Athenian standards he has failed dismally as a *kurios* ('legal guardian'), for he
was supposed to care for their future, provide them with a
dowry etc.[58] Again, contemporary norms are not simply to be
mapped directly onto the world of the stage, but Oedipus does
not attend adequately to his daughters' future. It is another
sign of the victory of community over family, and it is almost as
an afterthought that he recommends his daughters to Theseus'
protection (1631-5):

7. Characters

O dear head,
give to me the ancient[59] pledge of your hand for my children,
and you, children, to this man; and grant
that you will never willingly betray them, but complete whatever
you intend with good thought and expedience for them always.

This is small reward, and it ignores the fact that his actions towards his sons have doomed what is left of his family.[60] His daughters are essentially abandoned to the care of a mighty and faithful man (above, pp. 114-15), but someone beyond their kin and their community, whose connection is to Oedipus himself, and whose city is, because of this connection, opposed to the citizens of Thebes and the surviving members of the daughters' family. Despite his *philia*, and their *trophê* and *ponoi*, therefore, Antigone and Ismene are only marginally better off than the sons. Indeed, Antigone sums up their predicament in precisely these terms (1685-8):

For how, in what foreign
land or wave of the sea
wandering will we have
our ill-borne nursing (*trophan*) of life?

The present interpretation of Oedipus' behaviour is rather critical,[61] but the qualities focused on are noted by other characters throughout the play.[62] Antigone's attempt to persuade her father to listen to Polyneices is delivered in the knowledge that Oedipus will continue to apply to his son the revenge ethic he used against his parents in his first apology (see Chapter 4, p. 54), and her description of the situation is very apt (1192-1200):

Others too have bad children
and a *sharp temper*, but when they are advised
their natures are charmed by the spells of their loved ones.
And you, look to those things, not the present ones,
but the paternal and maternal pains you endured,
and if you see them, I know, *you will know how ill a result
accrues from an ill temper.*
For you have no small matters of rumination,
deprived of your unseeing eyes.

131

This 'sharp temper' (1193), resumed in the 'ill temper' (1198), is inextricably linked with his 'paternal and maternal pains' (1196); Oedipus' sufferings are his own, and inseparable from his temper. Oedipus himself had earlier admitted this, but applied it to the act of self-blinding (437-8), which is the only 'error' that he admits to, but it is surely not insignificant that it was an action of rage.[63] Prone to anger himself, Creon says (as we have seen, pp. 117-18) much the same thing of his kinsman (852-5) as does Theseus to Oedipus' description of Theban intentions (589-92):

> **Oed**. Those men will compel me to go there (Thebes).
> **Th.** But if you are willing, it's not good for you to flee.
> **Oed**. But, when *I* was willing, they did not permit it.
> **Th.** O foolish man, anger in evils is not sensible.

and, again, at his vehement refusal even to hear his son speak (1175-6). But the last word is set on Oedipus' character by his son. When he calls for his sister's aid for the 'hard to meet with, hard to address mouth of our father' (1276-7), when he speaks with resignation of his father's desire that his sons should die (1426), he knows that the old man's fury is undimmed and unquenchable. That Polyneices does not attempt to persuade Oedipus allows the poet to construct a sympathetic exchange with Antigone. Apart from its powerful contrast between Oedipus' and Antigone's attitudes to Polyneices, his son well recognises the strength of paternal curses (1432-4):

> Don't hold me back; but my concern will be this road,
> ill-fated and evil,
> at the hands of our father here and his Erinyes.

Oedipus has indeed become a personification of Eumenidean revenge (see Chapter 5, pp. 71-4), and it is therefore fitting that, immediately after Polyneices' exit, the play now moves towards the preternatural symbols of Oedipus' heroisation (1447ff.). He has cut himself entirely away from all the relationships which made him human – community, children, family – and deracinated himself for an existence in permanent cult (Chapter 5, pp. 79-85). His closest link is now with the *Semnai Theai*, in whose grove he disappears.

Oedipus is a mixture of extraordinary suffering and great power; a symbol of the dangers, as well as the powers, attendant on those beyond the usual run of mortal men; someone whose extreme, individual adherence to the 'help friends / harm enemies' ethic necessitates the suffering of those who have harmed and those who have helped. His hatreds and benefits can cover individuals, families and whole communities. In his concern for reputation, and unshakeable self-conviction, Oedipus gives place to no one, but the dynamic between his power and impotence drives his character throughout the play, for his qualities (intellect, command, control, perseverance) struggle against his reduction, and allow him eventually to transcend them – not triumph over, for Oedipus is translated from the limitations of human life to the power of an heroic cult.[64] There is no approval of his behaviour or attitudes, rather an acknowledgement that he cannot be incorporated within society. There is simply no other place for someone like Oedipus to go. Rehabilitation in human terms is impossible, a quiet death in peace inconceivable.[65] By virtue of the preternatural, explosive mixture of qualities which made him such a problematic figure in life, this ultimate suppliant becomes eventually Athens' great saviour in death.

8

Oedipal Receptions

No discussion of Athenian tragedy these days seems complete without an acknowledgement that the plays survived well beyond their original contexts.[1] Though it reveals less about Sophocles' work than the (re-)uses to which it has been put, the notion of 'reception' is not simply a modern academic fad. Indeed, the process began in the ancient period, where the play was read in an autobiographical manner to provide (or bolster) stories like that about Sophocles' trial for incompetence (Chapter 1, pp. 12-13). This particular tale was repeated well into the Roman period, and so autobiographism can be said to be one of the *OC*'s earliest reception themes.

The *OC* has inspired subsequent artists dealing with the same or similar material right into the modern period. One can contrast the efforts of three supreme poets – John Milton's *Samson Agonistes* (1671), a notable step in the *OT*'s Christianisation;[2] T.S. Eliot's drama *The Elder Statesman* (1958), which sees a corrupt old man face the errors of his youth and become redeemed;[3] and W.B. Yeats' translation of the *OC* (1934) – to see the evidence of Sophocles' continuing and varied influence. But this process had already begun in antiquity, with several (lost) Oedipus plays known to us from Athens and Rome,[4] though we can only speculate about the precise nature of the *OC*'s influence on them. Of course, the story contributed to a wealth of writing between antiquity and the medieval period about Oedipus, though other ancient texts (such as Statius' epic *Thebaid*) were perhaps more influential in this tradition.[5]

Returning specifically to the stage, the Archive of Performance of Greek and Roman Drama at Oxford University records 158 performances of works drawing to varying extents on the *OC* since 1776.[6] Some of these are considerable reworkings, as William Mason's *Caractacus* (Covent Garden, 6 December

1776),[7] which drew heavily on it but set the story in the context
of British resistance to the Roman army. Many other performances combine the *OC* with other 'Theban' plays, whether
creating a new dramatic whole or simply staging the works
sequentially, as (of the former group) Rudolf Walter's
Oidipodeia (Brno, 9 January 1926) or (of the latter) the Royal
Shakespeare Company's *The Thebans* (Stratford-upon-Avon,
1991).[8] Sequentialism has also found a home in the modern
media: BBC TV broadcast Don Taylor's translations in Septem-
ber 1986, starring John Gielgud as Teiresias, Anthony Quayle
as Oedipus, and Juliet Stevenson as Antigone,[9] while BBC
Radio 3 broadcast Robert Fagles' translations in 1984, with
Patrick Stewart as Creon and Tim Piggott-Smith as Oedipus.[10]
This modern phenomenon may have ancient precedent, with
some scholars arguing that the *OC* was performed together
with the *OT* and *Antigone* in 401 BC.[11] Certainly, the encyclo-
paedic need for 'the' complete story could be readily fostered by
the (original) intertextual relationships between the plays (see
Chapter 3, pp. 45-50), and so – while not necessarily Sophocles'
intention – these productions are not just a recent impulse or
misunderstanding of the dramatic dynamics in ancient Athens.
Even in that context, plays were not to be viewed in splendid
isolation, for the poets had to offer four works to get performance at the City Dionysia and, earlier in the century, it had been
the custom to present linked stories across the tetralogy.

The modern ideal of freestanding single performance is more
removed from Athenian experience, but it too has found a place
in the *OC*'s performance history. Though the *OT* was more
famous – perhaps explaining why so many modern performances of the *OC* are linked with other 'Oedipus plays' – there
have been many notable single productions of the *OC* (aside, of
course, from the many university productions around the world,
in both translation and ancient Greek): the National Theatre of
Greece's *Oidipous epi Kolono* (translation by Ioannis Gryparis)
toured the world for several years after its first performance at
Epidauros in 1958,[12] and again between 1975 and 1982;[13] BBC
Radio 3 broadcast a performance of Robert Fitzgerald's translation featuring Michael Redgrave as Oedipus, John Hurt as
Polyneices and Joss Ackland as Creon (19 March 1978);[14] Studio
Oyunculari's Turkish language production (Istanbul 2004)
emphasised, partly through lighting, the centrality of interro-

gation and trial so prominent in Sophocles' play;[15] and Klaus Michael Grüber's Burgtheater production (Vienna 2003) starred Bruno Ganz as Oedipus.[16]

The *OC* has also proven attractive for musical composition,[17] though none of these works forms a regular part of modern repertoires. Antonio Sacchini's *Oedipe à Colone* (libretto: Nicolas-François Guillard) premiered at Versailles in 1786,[18] Niccolò Zingarelli's *Edipo a Colono* (libretto: Simeone Antonio Sografi) at Venice in 1802,[19] Giacomo Rossini's incidental music for Giambattista Giusti's *Edipo a Colono* was written in Italy between 1813 and 1816,[20] Felix Mendelssohn's incidental music for Ludwig Tieck's *Ödipus auf Kolonos* opened at Berlin in 1845,[21] George Enescu's *Oedipe* (libretto: Edmund Fleg) at Paris in 1936,[22] and Theodoros Antoniou's *Oedipus at Colonus* (libretto: Giorgios Michailidis) at Athens in 1998.[23] Enescu's work, the only masterpiece of the bunch, is a story of Oedipus' whole life, with Act IV depending directly on the *OC*, though with notable changes: Creon offers the throne directly to Oedipus, thus removing the rather important exchange with Polyneices, and Oedipus' sight is restored as he leads Theseus off the stage. There is a strong redemptive element here – not at all unexampled in scholarly writing on the *OC*[24] – with even the Furies summoning Oedipus to a beatific vision of the afterlife. Sacchini's opera strikes a similar note, though somewhat differently: at the very end, Oedipus forgives Polyneices (who had already successfully approached Theseus as an ally against Eteocles) and so earns forgiveness from the gods, heralding the marriage of Polyneices and Eriphyle (Theseus' daughter).

But perhaps the most famous modern production is the *Gospel at Colonus*, a formally daring adaptation by Lee Breuer and Bob Telson set in a Pentecostal church in America.[25] This extremely successful work once more Christianises the story, using a painting of the Last Judgement as backdrop, and making its characters members of the church hierarchy. More explicitly figured as a prophet, Oedipus ascends to heaven in a state of grace; he is a more accepting figure, the question of his self-justification is almost entirely ignored, and Polyneices is marked as insincere. The *OC*'s emphasis on place is transformed into an exploration of home, exile and origin in the African-American experience, and the play's hopeful vision of the Athenian future is turned to the racial politics of modern America.

*

The *OC* has not proved to be the most popular of Sophocles' plays for reperformance, though it has a solid reception history. This may be attributed, in part, to a decreased interest in Sophocles as an historical figure, one of the strongest dynamics driving the play's reception in the ancient period. We might, in addition, factor in the greater prominence afforded the *Antigone* and (particularly) *OT* in the modern period, as an obstacle to the expansion of an already crowded repertoire. But perhaps most importantly, there is also a difficulty, for a modern (Christian) audience, in reconciling Oedipus' two sides – honoured by the gods and yet unable to transcend the faults of character which have dominated his life (hence, e.g., the alterations in his character in *Gospel at Colonus*). Sophocles' character cannot accept or approach the type of redemption evinced, for example, in Sacchini's opera, but our continued attempts to recreate Oedipus' story show his undimmed ability to fascinate us.

Notes

1. Sophocles and Athens

1. The materials are gathered in Radt (1999) 27-96 ('Testimonia'). The admirably succinct treatment by Lloyd-Jones (1994) 6-15 contrasts strongly with the rather credulous narrative (e.g.) in Webster (1936) 1-17. Also very useful are Easterling (2006a) 1-6 and Markantonatos (2007) 10-21.

2. See, e.g., Waldock (1951) 219-21; Calder (1985) 7.

3. Easterling (2006a) 7; also Lefkowitz (1978) 469.

4. Text in Radt (1999) 29-40; translation in Lefkowitz (1981) 160-3.

5. See Easterling (2006a) and, for the Roman period, Holford-Strevens (1999).

6. Attica was divided for administrative purposes into 'demes', which were the basic constituent of Athenian political structure, and could range tremendously in size, population and settlement pattern.

7. See Snell (1986) 132-5 for fragments and testimonia.

8. See Woodbury (1970) 213-15 for confusions in the sources.

9. See Jameson (1971) and, for further speculation, Calder (1985) 1-4.

10. Sommerstein (1985) ad loc., 165; Olson (1998) ad 698-9, 211; T 104; also below, n. 20.

11. See Heath (1997).

12. See Heath (1987b).

13. See Lefkowitz (1981) 84; *contra* e.g. Markantonatos (2007) 15-20.

14. See, e.g., Lefkowitz (1991). For deities appearing to the authors of poetic narratives, see, e.g., Pindar and Demeter and her request for a hymn, which he fulfils and augments by building an altar to her (fr. 37 S-M) (with Lekfowitz (1981) 60-1), or Pindar's 'meeting' with Alcmaeon in *Pythian* 8, or Helen and Stesichorus' *Palinode* (see Kelly (2007) with further references).

15. Cf. Kearns (1989) 20, 146. This should, as Pat Easterling reminds me, be linked with the way in which other poets were honoured as heroes, as e.g. Euripides at Salamis; see Lefkowitz (1981).

16. See Connolly (1998). Edmunds (1996) attempts to draw parallels between Sophocles' reception of Asclepius and Theseus' reception of Oedipus in the *OC*.

17. Cf. Seaford (1994a) 393-405, 129-39; also Harrison (1989).

18. For the *dikê paranoias* ('action for mental incapacity'), cf. Harrison (1968) 79-80. The passage in the *Life* is lacunose and troubled (cf. Radt (1999) ad loc., 35); see above, pp. 12-13 and below, n. 21.

19. Lefkowitz (1981) 84-5.

20. See above, n. 14. Halliwell (1982) 153 connects it with Aristophanes *Peace* 694-5 (above, n. 10).

21. Jebb (1900) xxxix-xli; also Radt (1999) 35.
22. See Snell (1986) 3-52.
23. T 1.76, ascribing the figure to Aristophanes of Byzantium, though adding that '17 are spurious'. The *Suda* gives 123 (T 2.9). The strike rate percentages above are calculated on the basis that the numbers need to be divided by four (three tragedies and a satyr play) in order to give the number of festivals at which the poet competed, but this procedure is open to objection: e.g. there were one-off plays, like Aeschylus' *Women of Aetna*.
24. Taplin (1977) 323 n. 3 suggests that there were never less than 15 members in a chorus.
25. A position convincingly demolished by van Erp Taalman Kip (1987) (with refs at 417-18 n. 1).
26. See, e.g., Podlecki (1966) 63-100.
27. See, e.g., Bowie (1997) 56-62, Calder (1971) and the wild speculation of Vickers (2008). For other 'political' interpretations, see Calder (1985) and Edmunds (1996) 87-146.
28. Wilamowitz (1917) 316-17; also Jebb (1900) xlii.
29. See Avezzù and Guidorizzi (2008) xxviii-xix. On the involvement of this Sophocles in performances at Eleusis, see Chapter 5, n. 62.
30. On the political associations of Colonus and the cult, see esp. Siewert (1979) and Edmunds (1996); also Chapter 5, pp. 68-9, and Chapter 6, pp. 92-5, 98-106.
31. Campbell (1891) 209; also Campbell (1879) 275-9.
32. See Jebb (1900) xlii.
33. See Seaford (1994a) 123-39; Avezzu and Guidorizzi (2008) 261-2. In her forthcoming commentary, Pat Easterling plausibly relates the passage to the knowledge which the Thebans and Ismene could reasonably have at this point in the action, and therefore interprets the verb as referring to an intended moment of sacrifice.
34. See Spence (1993) 20-1, 98-101, 126-33, esp. 132-3; also Lardinois (1992) 324 and n. 37.
35. See, e.g., Markantonatos (2007) 36.
36. Hanson (1983); also Chapter 6, pp. 102-6.
37. *contra*, e.g., Knox (1964) 143: 'But [Sophocles] knew already, as all the world must have known, that Athens had lost the war.'
38. See Rhodes (2006) chs 11-15.
39. See Rhodes (2006) ch. 13.
40. For accounts of the festival, cf. esp. Pickard-Cambridge (1968) 57-125; Csapo and Slater (1995) 103-21; also Goldhill (1987) 58-68. Osborne (1993) gives an excellent introduction to the Athenian festival year.
41. See esp. van Erp Taalman Kip (1987) 416.
42. See Allen and Story (2005) 14-16.
43. See Wilson (2000) esp. 144-99; also Pickard-Cambridge (1968) 90 (on the latter point).
44. See the new study in Wilson (2008).
45. Athenian choruses also competed in contests for 'dithyrambic' poetry (a type of metrically and musically complex verse narrating mythical

events), which drew famous artists from all over the Greek world and offered tremendously valuable prizes; see Pickard-Cambridge (1968) 74-9; also id. (1962) 31-8; D'Angour (1997) 334-43, 346-50.

46. See Taplin (1999) 35.

47. See Pickard-Cambridge (1968) 68-70.

48. See Heath (1987b).

49. See Edmunds (1996).

50. See Wilson (1997) (and those cited by Markantonatos (2007) 13 n. 9).

51. See Easterling (1999) 101-2; also Chapter 5, pp. 81-4.

52. Of course, Aeschylus' *Persians* (472 BC) is the obvious exception (for others, see Sourvinou-Inwood (2003) 16-19), yet even in this near-contemporary play, the Persian royal household looks like nothing so much as a Greek royal household; their experience – *hybris* overtaken by disaster – is that experienced again and again by Greek heroes and kings in tragedy. The play provides neither an illustration of an ultimately preclusive and unrelatable 'Other', nor a subversive attempt to elide categories of Greek and non-Greek, but a demonstration that the non-Greek 'barbarians' of the audience's present are in many ways extremely like the Greeks of the audience's past.

53. Fragments and testimonia in Snell (1986) 69-79. The two dates represent his first victory (T 1.3), and a production in which Themistocles was his *khorêgos* ('producer' / 'financier') (T 4); for his *Capture of Miletus*, see esp. Rosenbloom (1993).

54. See, e.g., Knox (1964) 143, 155; also Chapter 7, pp. 110-16.

55. This is particularly associated with Simon Goldhill and the contributors to Winkler and Zeitlin (1990), roundly criticised by Griffin (1998), Friedrich (1996) and Seaford (1996). The idea that democratic discourse operates by encouraging its citizens to challenge its central values is now a scholarly commonplace: see, e.g., Euben (1986) 24; Heiden (1993) esp. 164-5 and 165 n. 40; Croally (1994) 45; Pelling (1997b) 224-35.

56. See esp. *Laws* 700e-701b; *Gorgias* 502b-d; also *Rep.* 604e, *Apol.* 22a-b, *Rep.* 605c-d.

57. See Csapo (2007) 96-100.

58. See, in particular, the works of Christiane Sourvinou-Inwood and Richard Seaford.

59. See, e.g., Taplin (1999); Allan (2001a).

2. A Synopsis of the Play

1. See Arnott (1962) 1-41; Taplin (1980) 7-11; Rehm (1992) 34-6; Csapo and Slater (1995) 79-81; Wiles (2000) 104-9; Csapo (2007). In this chapter I use only the term 'acting area' with no implications as to its position, size, or relationship with the orchestra. In the rest of the book, however, I deploy the term 'stage' as a metaphor for the world of the heroes within tragedy, with no implication about the actual acting area.

2. See Taplin (1983); Wiles (1997) 133-60, esp. 146 n. 53.

3. See above, n. 1, with Pickard-Cambridge (1968), Scullion (1994), Rehm (2002) 1-62.

4. See below, n. 8.

5. Following the now standard divisions put forth in the twelfth chapter of Aristotle's *Poetics*, I use the term *prologos* to denote everything before the entry song of the chorus (which is called the *parodos*); scenes between choral songs (*stasima*) are called *episodes*, and everything after the last of these *stasima* is the *exodos*; the scheme adopted here is basically that of Jebb (1900) 9 (see also Kamerbeek (1984) 6-14), though I use *kommos* only for lyrical dialogue containing lamentation, and *amoibaion* for all other such dialogues. On the absolute artificiality of these terms, see esp. Taplin (1977) 49-60, 470-6.

6. Dramaturgy is always controversial and uncertain; cf. Jebb (1900) xxxvii-viii; Arnott (1962) 35f., 99f.; Seale (1982) 113-43; Taplin (1983) 158-63; Dunn (1992) 1-9; Wiles (1997) 146-51. I do not speculate here on choral choreography; see Rehm (1992) 54-7 for brief remarks.

7. See Taplin (1977) 336, 455 n. 2 (also (1983) 183); *contra* Jebb (1900) xxxvii. I assume here that the *skênê* was used for entrances and exits, though that must remain conjectural.

8. This may be a second stone seat on the stage, situated outside the grove (so Jebb (1900) xxxviii (with diagram); Markantonatos (2007) 82), or the edge of a rocky ledge (so Lloyd-Jones (1994) 435); see also Kamerbeek (1984) ad 192-3, 49), or simply the same stage prop as before (*OC* 19), which now represents another outcrop (see Wiles (1997) 188). For a discussion of the rock and its dramaturgic possibilities, see Allison (1984) 72-3; Budelmann (2000b); also Chapter 5, pp. 81-2, and Chapter 6, pp. 101-2.

9. Wiles (1997) 146 argues that she goes to the left side of the stage, since she is later seized by Thebans from that direction.

10. This is the first of three scenes in the play in which four characters are on stage – though only three of them speak – Oedipus, Antigone, Theseus and (the silent) Ismene; in the first part of the fourth episode there are Polyneices, Oedipus, Antigone and (again silent) Ismene; in the second part of the fourth episode, Oedipus, Theseus, Antigone and (again silent) Ismene. It is a convention of Athenian tragedy, known as the 'three actor rule', that only three actors (i.e. with speaking roles) are used in any production; see Pickard-Cambridge (1968) 135-56. This could be preserved here, for the fourth figure in these scenes is always mute, though it would result in some juggling of the roles; for their division, cf. Campbell (1879) 284; Jebb (1900) 7-8; Pickard-Cambridge (1968) 142-4; Kamerbeek (1984) 23.

11. See Taplin (1983) 159-60; *contra* Jebb (1900) ad loc., 199.

12. Jebb (1900) 239 has him moving to the left of the stage. For the exit into the *skênê*, see Taplin (1983) 182-3; Seale (1982) 118; Wiles (1997) 165-6. One might propose also an exit to the right (as, e.g., Schunck (1907) 75), symbolising Athenian territory, adding visually to the textual ambiguities over the precise location of Oedipus' tomb. If this is right, then some or all of the subsequent arrivals – of the messenger (1579f.), the daughters (1667f.) and Theseus himself (1751f.) – would come from the audience's right (as, e.g., Jebb (1900) 269). Indeed, even if the exit here is into the *skênê*, these several subsequent entries might come from the audience's right anyway, emphasising the assumption of Oedipus into Attic territory.

13. It is not clear if Antigone and Ismene depart for Thebes immediately (so, e.g., Burian (1974) 427; Seale (1982) 138; Taplin (1983) 163), or if they follow Theseus back towards Athens, with the journey to Thebes postponed. Certainly it would be visually powerful were they to exit left straightaway, and so follow Creon and Polyneices at once to doom and disaster, as opposed to departing with Theseus and the Attic chorus, who leave to the right and the promise of a better future.

14. For a complete breakdown of the metres used in the song portions of the *OC*, see Dawe (1996) 91-8; Avezzù and Guidorizzi (2008) 387-403. For a somewhat speculative discussion of their effects, see Scott (1996) xiii-xix, 196-253.

15. Michaelides (1978) s.v., 305.

3. The Oedipus Myth and the *OC*

1. See, e.g., Robert (1915); Edmunds (1981); March (1987) 121-54; Mastronarde (1994) 17-30; Segal (2001) 24-48; Markantonatos (2007) 41-70. For a general introduction, see Burian (1997a).

2. Cf. the contest between 'Aeschylus' and 'Euripides' in Aristophanes' *Frogs* (405 BC), when the former refuses to suspend his disbelief as he listens to his opponent's quotations from the now lost *Antigone*, and instead uses his own knowledge of the story in order to pour scorn on Euripides' version (1182-95).

3. On the asterisk used here, see above, pp. 40-1.

4. Sommerstein (1995-6) argues that Polyneices was the elder brother in the early epic sources.

5. March (1987) 138, criticised e.g. by Mastronarde (1994) 18 n. 1; see also Markantonatos (2007) 52.

6. See Zeitlin (1990). One can exaggerate this, as royal houses in other Greek cities found themselves depicted in similarly unpleasant situations, and Thebes was anyway heavily represented in heroic myth. Moreover, Theseus in the *OC* makes a point of disassociating Thebes from the the bad behaviour of Creon (919); see Mills (1997) 180.

7. Oedipus becomes furious at Creon for, among other things, mentioning his sister's misfortune (978-87). It is a feature of Athenian culture that the names (and reputations) of female relatives were protected, even in court cases where they were intimately involved; see Just (1989) 27-8.

8. See West (1999) 39-44; Lloyd-Jones (2002); Sewell-Rutter (2007) 61-7.

9. This had proven to be a fruitful development in the *OT* as well; in shifting the location of the meeting between Oedipus and Laius from Potniae (as in Aeschylus' Theban trilogy; see Hutchinson (1985) xix-xx; Aeschylus F 387a Radt) to the 'three ways' near Daulia in Phocis (*OT* 733-4), Sophocles brought Delphi and Apollo's warning more fully into the story (i.e. beyond the fact of warning), and he was followed by Euripides in the *Phoenician Women* (38 etc.).

10. See also Aeschylus *Seven Against Thebes* 778-87f., with Hutchinson (1985) xxiv-v.

11. See, e.g., Σ *OC* 1375; Mueller-Goldingen (1985) 273-4. One might, however, consider the sons' transgressions in the light of the importance of hospitality in the epic world, and the paramount need to divide 'honour portions' in the proper way; see also Edmunds (1981) 229 n. 31; Seaford (1994a) 126-39.

12. See Jebb (1900) ad *OC* 1375, 212-13; Avezzù and Guidorizzi (2008) ad *OC* 421-2, 262-3; ad 1375, 359.

13. See Chapter 4.

14. See Blundell (1989) 258 n. 116; also Rosenmeyer (1952) 108 n. 67.

15. This poem was composed in honour of Arcesilas IV of Cyrene, and (at its end) Pindar pleads for the return from exile of a certain Damophilus, whose circumstance is expressed by an allegory introduced by the injunction 'and now understand the wisdom of Oedipus' (263). The following sentence concerns an oak stripped of its finery which is still useful for several purposes, even in 'alien halls' (268); though Oedipus could be introduced here only as a byword for understanding such riddles, the suggestion of Damophilus' exile could also be applied to the story of the wandering Oedipus himself. Edmunds (1981) contends that the identity of Oedipus as a wandering figure is more essentially related to his cult status, and could well be very old. However that may be, the earliest *explicit* extant statement of his exile comes in the *OT*.

16. The play is undated, though conventionally placed *c.* 411-409 BC; see Mastronarde (1994) 11-14. These lines have themselves been suspected; see Mastronarde (1994) ad loc., 626; Mills (1997) 161-3. Pat Easterling suggests to me that Euripides may well have known what Sophocles was, or was intending to do, with the Oedipus legend. For another indication that Oedipus' association with Athens predates the *OC* (and the *Phoenician Women*), see Euripides F 554b Kannicht (= Menander *Samia* 325-6) with Collard (2005) 60-2. Seaford (1994b) 287 has suggested that Aeschylus' *Oedipus* (performed as part of the tetralogy (467 BC) to which *Seven against Thebes* belonged) ended with the establishment of Oedipus' cult at Colonus.

17. Σ *Od.* 11.271 (= Androtion *FGrH* 324 F 62).

18. Σ *OC* 91 (= Lysimachus *FGrH* 382 F 2).

19. Lardinois (1992) 325-6 deems the Eteonos tradition a Theban story.

20. See Edmunds (1981) 223-4; Lardinois (1992).

21. See Kearns (1989) 50-2, 208-9; also Chapter 5, pp. 81-3.

22. King of Argos, and a member of the expedition which attacks Thebes with Polyneices, he is the only one to survive the assault.

23. Cf. Kearns (1989) 208-9, who denies the possibility of two contemporary cults, and opts for the Colonan cult. Kirsten (1973) reverses Kearns' conclusion, but there is too little material to be certain either way.

24. See Chapter 6, pp. 100-2.

25. See Jebb (1900) xxxv. Linforth (1951) 172-4 suggests, plausibly, that the inconsistency reflects the fact Oedipus does not know the precise manner of his death.

26. See Scullion (1999) 228. On tragedy and cultic reality, see esp. Krummen (1993).

27. The first and third of these features are mentioned by Pausanias (1.28.6), the second by Σ *OC* 1600 (though the temple there belongs to Demeter *Khlous* – 'of the shoot'). One might also remember that Creon foregrounds the Areopagus when speaking of the court named after it (947-9). Though it could suggest a link between the grove and his tomb, the language of Oedipus' original statement about his relationship with the Eumenides (89-91) is sufficiently vague not to demand the association.

28. For the other advantage – blurring of Colonus and Athens – see Chapter 6, pp. 98-106.

29. See Dunn (1996); Scullion (1999); also Reinhardt (1979) 193 (= (1947) 202).

30. This section owes almost everything in it to Seidensticker (1972) = (2005) and Bernard (2001) 58-83; see also Jebb (1900) ix-x, xxi-ii; Burian (1974) 429; Kamerbeek (1984) 3-6; Segal (2001) 131-43; Markantonatos (2007) 195-230.

31. See the opening sentence of the *OC*'s first hypothesis: 'the *Oedipus at Colonus* is in some way joined with the *Tyrannus*'.

32. Jebb (1902) xxix-xxx; Kamerbeek (1967) 28-9; Seidensticker (1972) 255 n. 5 = (2005) 1 n. 5; Müller (1984); Dawe (2006) ad *OT* 1515-30, 200-1. See, e.g., Hester (1984) 21-3, March (1987) 148-54 and Müller (1996) = (1999) for the (to my mind unconvincing, but increasingly popular) thesis that some portions of the *OC* (and Sophocles' other Theban plays) were composed, after Sophocles' death, for a performance of the *OT*, *OC* and *Antigone* in 401 BC.

33. See Collard (2005) 60-1 for Euripides' *Oedipus*.

34. Bernard (2001) 60-3, among others, argues that the *OT* is so insistent about exile that no one could doubt its long-term postponement at the end of that play; cf. also Mills (1997) 161.

35. The ending of the *OT* is an enormous problem, but I follow Davies (1983) in seeing here a continuity in Oedipus' reluctance to release his control over events, and Creon's behaviour as a sensible desire to consult Apollo after this unexpected turn of events; cf., *contra*, e.g., Hester (1984). The arguments of Dawe (2006) 192-203 against the passage's authenticity are answered by Finglass (2009). For further discussion of the two passages above, see Chapter 4, pp. 60-1.

36. i.e. about his identity, the parricide and the incest.

37. See Shields (1961) and Chapter 5, pp. 65-8 for his 'special sight'.

38. Burian (1974) 429; Seidensticker (1972) 265-6 = (2005) 16-17. Of course, we only have seven plays out of Sophocles' total output, and cannot be sure that this would not have been a more common practice (indeed, Athene's opening speech in the *Ajax* is also 13 verses long).

39. Theseus had already promised to make Oedipus 'the lord of his daughters' (1041), a promise he later refers to as an 'oath' (1145-6). His acceptance of Oedipus' supplication extends his protection to the daughters as well. Perhaps this is why Oedipus refers to Theseus' 'ancient pledge' (*pistin arkhaian* OC 1632); *contra* Jebb (1900) ad loc., 252-2, who prints *horkian* ('with an oath') for *arkhaian* ('ancient').

40. See Chapter 7, pp. 116-18.

41. Seidensticker (1972) 269 = (2005) 22.

42. See Winnington-Ingram (1980) 274-5; Bernard (2001) 159-68; Markantonatos (2007) 216-24.

43. See esp. Mueller-Goldingen (1985) 272-9; also Calder (1985) 4-6. Nor are these the only plays to be invoked. There were at least seven other plays titled 'Oedipus' performed in fifth-century Athens, one by Aeschylus and one by Euripides, and Theban myth was an extremely popular source for Athenian tragedians.

44. See Chapter 2, p. 34 and n. 13, for the possibility that they actually depart for Thebes at the end of the *OC*.

45. Several scholars have seen no link with the *Antigone* here (e.g., Wilamowitz (1917) 331-2, 367; Waldock (1951) 225-6).

46. Burton (1980) 271 terms the *OC*'s ending a 'recapitulation in miniature' of the *Antigone*'s opening scene.

47. Bernard (2001) 163-4; also Chapter 7, p. 110. Pat Easterling suggests to me that much more importance could be placed on the *Antigone*, given the importance of her role in the *OC* (clear from the opening line of the play) and the fame of her character.

48. Calder (1985) 5.

49. See also Wilamowitz (1917) 362.

4. Oedipal Accounts

1. See, e.g., Seidensticker (1972) 263 n. 1; Bernard (2001) 104-5, esp. nn. 169-70. In Athenian legal practice homicide (in its varying forms) had nothing to do with 'subjective' or 'objective' innocence (*pace* Cairns (1993) 222 n. 19), for the fundamental anachronism of which, see esp. Bernard (2001) 104-21.

2. See MacDowell (1963); Harrison (1971) 36-43 (procedure); also MacDowell (1978) 113-18 (types of homicide), 118-22 (procedure); Phillips 2008 (59-61). Some have attempted to view Oedipus' case directly in contemporary legal terms: see below, nn. 20 and 21.

3. See, in general, Parker (1983) ch. 4; MacDowell (1963) 3-5, 141-50; Phillips (2008) 62-3.

4. See MacDowell (1963) 116, though the legal process is actually rather uncertain: Gagarin (2002) 58 n. 2 doubts whether it was legally punishable in Athens; Ostwald (1986) 6 explicitly denies it; Phillips (2008) 106-7 suggests that it could be prosecuted also by a charge of impiety (if the prosecutor were unrelated).

5. See Harrison (1968) 21-3, esp. 22-3 n. 3; also Cohen (1991) 225-7.

6. See Avezzù and Guidorizzi (2008) ad 87, 221.

7. See Chapter 3, p. 39 and n. 8, for the possibility that other crimes are to be inferred in the play.
   8. See MacDowell (1963) 75-6. This type of killing was within the jurisdiction of a third court in Athens, the Delphinion, on which see MacDowell (1963) 70-81.
   9. Misread by Avezzù and Guidorizzi (2008) ad 548, 271-2.
   10. See esp. Winnington-Ingram (1980) 261f., though he assumes a reference to the *OT*, and does not mention Oedipus' admission there that Laius 'in no way paid an even penalty' (810) for his attack.
   11. At 521, for instance, the OCT reads 'I endured these worst of things, strangers, I endured them *willingly*, let the god know; | but none of these things was my choice.' The MSS, however, read *unwillingly* (unmetrical) and several editors have proposed different readings. Again, at 525, the OCT reads: 'with an ill wedlock, the city bound me, *knowing nothing*, to the doom arising from my marriage,' while the MSS make the words 'knowing nothing' apply to the city and not to Oedipus. Finally, at 547-8 Oedipus in the OCT says 'seized by doom I murdered and destroyed | but in law I am pure; unknowing I came to this', while the MSS read for the first line 'for I have murdered and killed others', which makes a considerable change to the argument Oedipus is trying to make.
   12. See Chapter 7, p. 114 and n. 14.
   13. See MacDowell (1963) 70-81 for self-defence; also above, pp. 56-9.
   14. See Gagarin (2002) 58 n. 2.
   15. See above, n. 11.
   16. Pat Easterling suggests to me that we also need to consider the psychological advantages of this passage, specifically for an actor considering how to express Oedipus' process of coping with his actions.
   17. See Halliwell (1997) 138-40; also Long (1968) 159.
   18. See above, Chapter 3, pp. 45-9.
   19. See MacDowell (1963) 70-81.
   20. Finkelberg (1997) 572 would apply the strictures of Plato *Laws* 869bc, according to which self-defence would not avail a parricide, thus explaining Oedipus' use of the ignorance criterion. However, this is one of a series of proposals for an ideal state, *not* a direct reflection of Athenian law, and falls within the section of the *Laws* on 'homicide in anger', which was not a category recognised in Athens.
   21. Edmunds (1996) 134-8 argues that Oedipus' description of the act as *âkôn* amounts to an admission of guilt to a charge of *âkôn* homicide and a readiness to undergo exile. But Oedipus holds his exile against all those he views as responsible, refuses to admit any substantive wrongdoing on his part, and his self-defence plea makes this *not* a case of *âkôn* homicide.
   22. There may be other allusions to Athenian legal practice. For instance, Oedipus says that his father's soul would not speak against him (998-9), which may be an allusion to the custom that a killer could be absolved if the victim forgave him before death (MacDowell (1963) 8), although the second century AD grammarian Pollux (8.117) states explicitly

that this was not open to Athenian parricides. If trustworthy, this would show Oedipus yet again using legal criteria in a confused manner.

23. See Rosenmeyer (1952) 97-8.

24. As Pat Easterling points out to me, this was not always the case, and Polyneices at least seems sincere in his desire to bring his father back (1342-3), but he is also aware of the new oracle (1331-2), and both Oedipus (and then Theseus) seem to accept that his parricide (601) is the determinative consideration in the present circumstances.

25. See Chapter 3, pp. 45-9.

26. See Rosenmeyer (1952) 97; also above, pp. 54, 58.

27. On this theme, see Chapter 7, p. 123.

28. On this theme, see pp. 62-3.

29. Jebb (1900) ad loc., 73; *contra* Blundell (1989) 244 n. 57 and Easterling (forthcoming commentary).

30. See Easterling (1967) 9.

31. See above, pp. 54, 55-6, 57-8, on his marriage to Jocasta.

32. See Rosenmeyer (1952) 97.

33. See Chapter 5, pp. 59-62.

5. Oedipus and the Gods

1. See Linforth (1951); Parker (1999); Budelmann (2000a) esp. 133-9.

2. See Chapter 3, pp. 45-9 for the *OT* intertext, and pp. 39-40 for oracular novelties.

3. See Chapter 3, pp. 39-40; also Chapter 4, pp. 59-62.

4. See particularly Knox (1964); Garland (1985) 88; Bushnell (1988) 86-107; *contra* Bernard (2001) 98-102.

5. See Linforth (1951) 88 (also 82-92). His predictions of the reciprocal slaying of his sons (789-90, 1387-8) might go beyond this information, Antigone referring to them as 'oracles' (*mantuemath'* 1425) and 'oracular pronouncements' (*ethespisen* 1428). But it is better to relate this knowledge to Oedipus' desire for the most appalling and punishing form of kin-killing; see Linforth (1951) 110-11; also Bushnell (1988) 98-101.

6. To avoid duplication, I deal with the major examples of this divine topography (in the case of other deities) when discussing the chorus, whose first and second *stasima* (the 'Colonus' and 'Battle' odes) focus on the landscape of Athens in these terms; see Chapter 6, pp. 92-6.

7. A larger group may be suggested when Theseus sends men to summon those at the altar, 'both unhorsed and horsed' (899).

8. This reading (*parapetomena*) is an emendation in the OCT; the majority of MSS read 'fitted to' or 'plied by' (*paraptomena*), which would make the nature of Poseidon's gift to the Athenians all the clearer.

9. Stinton (1976) 325-6 (= (1990) 266-7) suggests also that the 'bridle' (714) is also a riddling allusion to the anchor, thus furthering the connection (and its blurring of provinces) between the cavalry and the navy. Stinton (328 = 269) also sees in the 'oar' a reference to the Argo, which was 'inspired by Athene and dedicated to Poseidon'.

10. On political harmony in the *OC*, see Chapter 6, pp. 98-106.
11. See 310 (Antigone reacting to the appearance of Ismene), 623 (chorus reacting to Oedipus' family history), 1456, 1471, 1485 (chorus crying out in fear of the thunder), 1749 (Antigone wondering where she is to go now).
12. See Budelmann (2000a) 150-2. For other cases, see 881-2, 1370-82, 1480-5, 1748-50.
13. See also 1435 (Polyneices' prayer for Antigone and Ismene).
14. For other examples, see 1267 ('Shame' sits beside Zeus), 1767, ('Oath' is the son of Zeus).
15. See Chapter 6, pp. 94-5.
16. This phrase is usually taken to refer to Hades but, given his prominence here, I prefer to refer it to Olympian Zeus 'acting on' or 'with regard to' the earth (West (1978) on *WD* 465, 276).
17. Kirkwood (1956) 219 argues that the phrase 'you here, you' strikes a particularly colloquial tone, suggesting a familiarity and sympathy between god and man that reflects the coming change in Oedipus' status. Bernard (2001) 154-5 feels that its more usual sense is abrupt and rude.
18. Easterling (2006c) 136 wisely comments, 'critics have thought of Hermes, Apollo, Zeus Chthonios, Persephone, or even Charon, but the whole point is that both narrator and audience can only guess who it belongs to'.
19. See Chapter 2, p. 26.
20. See Henrichs (1994) 49.
21. Cf. Linforth (1951) 92-7 (much too restrictive); Winnington-Ingram (1980) 264-72 (&f.); Edmunds (1981) 227f.; Blundell (1989) 256-8; Henrichs (1994); Edmunds (1996) 138-42.
22. See Henrichs (1994) 28.
23. The Colonan cult is also combined with that of the *Semnai Theai* on the Acropolis; cf. Chapter 6, p. 100.
24. Winnington-Ingram (1980) 275.
25. See Chapter 3, pp. 40-1. Mills (1997) 168 n. 28 links the curses at 1375-6 with the Erinyes, because the word for curses (*arai*) is another name for the Eumenides in Aeschylus (*Eum.* 417).
26. Henrichs (1983).
27. Winnington-Ingram (1980) 268.
28. Budelmann (2000b) n. 17.
29. On the theme of sight and blindness, see Chapter 3, p. 47 and n. 37.
30. See Fraenkel (1950) ad *Agamemnon* 1501, 711-12.
31. There is also the interrupted sacrifice to Poseidon conducted by Theseus, but the parallels between the two rites above seem more prominent; see Jouanna (1995). On supplication in general, see above, pp. 75-9.
32. See Chapter 7, pp. 122-3 for the 'teaching' theme.
33. Parker (1983) 107.
34. See Chapter 4, p. 55 for Oedipus' claims to purity.
35. Jouanna (1995) 50-1. Linforth (1951) 95, Zak (1995) 266f. and Bernard (2001) 143-8 stress that the rite's performance is not described, so

the Eumenides give no sign of their approval or friendship to Oedipus, and they conclude (too pessimistically) that they are angry with him.

36. Retaining the MSS' reading against the OCT, which prints 'nor with speech' (1653), and 'at the same time' (1655).

37. See Linforth (1951) 100-4; Winnington-Ingram (1980) 255; Vidal-Naquet (1988) 350; Blundell (1989) 254-6. Calame (1998) argues that Oedipus is to be viewed as mystic initiate; see above, pp. 81-2.

38. See, e.g., Linforth (1951) 103-4ff., 114-29, 187-91; Blundell (1989) 253-9.

39. Too daring for the editors of the OCT (among others), who change the reading to refer the word 'saving' to the Eumenides, invoked in the previous line and exhorted to 'receive' Oedipus'. Yet he characterises himself as a saviour to the chorus (460), and they repeat it back to him almost immediately (462-3); see Avezzù and Guidorizzi (2008) 68.

40. Burian (1974) 409.

41. See Gould (1973) = (2001).

42. Sinn (1993) 92.

43. See Heath (1987a) 65 and n. 52.

44. These are exceptions to the general rule that tragic myths are set somewhere other than Athens; see Sourvinou-Inwood (2003) 16-19. The city also figures in this role in other plays, such as Euripides' *Heracles mainomenos*, where Theseus invites the polluted Heracles to settle there after murdering his family.

45. Burian (1974) 415.

46. See Cairns (1993) 221. In fact, Oedipus never appeals to *aidôs*, though Antigone does to the chorus on his behalf (247) and to Oedipus on Polyneices' behalf (1192), and Polyneices attempts to deploy it with Oedipus (1268).

47. Cf. Jouanna (1995) 56.

48. Blundell (1989) 230-1 also notes the lack of formal supplication elements, but relates that to the establishment of *philia* between the two men, downplaying Theseus' calculation. As her own discussion of the institution makes clear, however, *philia* is no mere emotional attachment. Mills (1997) 171 suggests that Theseus accepts Oedipus without knowing of his benefit, but this is to ignore, firstly, the chorus' report that the stranger who had fetched them (and to whom Oedipus had made the first statement of his power (72 and 74) in the context of requesting Theseus' presence) had also gone to get Theseus (297-8). Secondly, Theseus only accepts Oedipus at 631ff., *after* hearing of the benefit and questioning him closely about its nature.

49. The word for 'citizen' is *empolin*, a conjecture for the MSS' *empalin* ('back'). *empolin* is again used at 1156 in order to distinguish a fellow citizen from a family member, and is generally judged a certain correction; *contra* Wilson (1997) 63-90.

50. See Krummen (1993) 196f.; cf. also Winnington-Ingram (1980) 261f.

51. Mills (1997) 166f. emphasises the risk inherent in receiving Oedipus, and so the level of his reward is an index of that risk and Theseus' calculation.

52. Garvie (2005) 79. Easterling (1967) 7 thinks the rejection deserved.

53. There is an intertextual reference here, to Aeschylus' *Seven against Thebes* (467 BC), in which the list of Argive allies is enumerated as Eteocles chooses a Theban warrior to match each Argive, who are slain to a man.

54. For Oedipus' shaping of this benefit as an expression of his character and his rhetorical strategies, see Chapter 7, pp. 121-33.

55. For an introduction to hero cult in Attica, see Parker (1996) 33-9, 282-3; Farnell (1921) 343f.; Kearns (1989); Seaford (1994a) 106-20. For tragedy, see Seaford (1994a) esp. 123-39; *contra* Linforth (1951) 97-104.

56. See Currie (2005) 87-157 (and 158-200 on the heroisation of the recently dead).

57. See Kearns (1989) 80.

58. See Kearns (1989) 44-54.

59. Contrast the minimalism of Griffin (1998) with the expansive attitude of Seaford (2000).

60. See Seaford (1994a) 127-8; Kearns (1989) 51-2; Edmunds (1996) 97-100; also Chapter 3, pp. 41-5, for the argument that secrecy and indirection also served the purpose of allowing Sophocles to harmonise (probably contemporary) divergent traditions about the location of his Athenian cults.

61. See Garland (1985) 61-2; Vickers (2008) 101-2; also Burkert (1987) more generally.

62. Colchester (1942) 24-7; Calame (1998); Markantonatos (2002) 197-220. We might remember that Sophocles (probably the grandson, who put on the *OC* in 401 BC) put on performances at the Dionysia in Eleusis; see *IG* II^2 3090 with Clinton (1992) 125 n. 22.

63. See Burkert (1985); also Richardson (1974) 188-9.

64. Richardson (1974) 22.

65. Edmunds (1981), (1996); Calame (1998); cf. also Markantonatos (2002) 197-220.

66. Easterling (2006c) 144.

67. See, e.g., Minadeo (1994) 159; Markantonatos (2002) 219: *contra*, Blundell (1989) 253-9.

68. See Easterling (2006c); *contra* Colchester (1942); cf. Zak (1995) 255-75 and Bernard (2001) 148-59, both of whom interpret Oedipus' end much more negatively, driven (perhaps too far) by the laudable aim to show that Oedipus' actions and attitudes are not to be approved.

69. After all, Ajax in his play has no conception that he is to be so honoured, and Eurystheus' description of his cult in the *Children of Heracles* does not match any historically recorded institution; see Kearns (1989) 49-50, 164; also Allan (2001b) 218-19.

70. See Scullion (1999).

71. See Kirkwood (1958) 244; Segal (1981) 380-2; Blundell (1989) 32f..

72. This reading (*xun' apokeitai*) is not that chosen in the OCT (*nux apokeitai*), which would mean 'one must not weep for those who have the night of the earth as their *kharis*'; see Jebb (1900) ad loc., 268; Seaford (1994a) 135 n. 141.

73. Blundell (1993) 306; Parker (1996) 130 and nn. 30-1.
74. Easterling (1999) 101-2; see Chapter 7, pp. 114-15.
75. Easterling (2006c); also above, pp. 80-2.
76. See Wallace (1979) 40; also Chapter 7, pp. 126-7.
77. See Chapter 1, pp. 14-18; also Chapter 6, pp. 102-6.
78. See Kirkwood (1986) 113.
79. See the review in Bernard (2001) 171-86.

6. Athens and Attica

1. For Sophocles' choruses (*OC* and elsewhere), cf. McDevitt (1972); Burton (1980); Gardiner (1987); Rosenmeyer (1993); Esposito (1996); Scott (1996); Travis (1999); Budelmann (2000a) 195-206; Markantonatos (2002) 179-97; Singh Dugha (2005).
2. See Taplin (1977) 323 n. 3.
3. See Murray and Wilson (2004); also Kowalzig (2007) 4-6.
4. *contra* Esposito (1996) and Singh Dhuga (2005), who grant the chorus great authority.
5. See esp. Gardiner (1987) 109-10; Taplin (1985).
6. *contra* Esposito (1996) 107; Singh Dhuga (2005) 338.
7. See Gardiner (1987) 110, 113-14.
8. Blundell (1993) 298.
9. See Chapter 4, pp. 55-6, 57-9.
10. Burton (1980) 261.
11. See Blundell (1993) 293f.
12. Singh Dhuga (2005) 339 bafflingly refers 'authority' to the chorus itself.
13. See Sourvinou-Inwood (1995) 393-8, esp. 394-5.
14. See Chapter 5, pp. 81-3.
15. The phrase might refer to Demeter and Persephone, invoked earlier (683 and 1050-3); see Chapter 5, pp. 81-3 for their possible connection with the hero cult of Oedipus.
16. The term *xenos* is frequently used of Oedipus in the *OC* (by the Athenian stranger 75; continually by the chorus 161, 184, 215, 492, 510, 518, 831 etc.; by Theseus 562-3; Creon 745; Polyneices 1335), and the fact that it means both 'foreigner' and 'guest' encapsulates well his simultaneous alterity and belonging to Athens.
17. See Winnington-Ingram (1980) 251 n. 9; Davidson (1986).
18. See Jebb (1900) Appendix, 286-8.
19. See Chapter 5, pp. 81-3.
20. See McDevitt (1972).
21. Suksi (2001) argues that it alludes to the story of Procne, who was transformed into a nightingale, and so foreshadows divine pity for Oedipus and his subsequent transformation. McDevitt (1972) 230-2 connects the bird with lamentation and death (though that seems a secondary connotation in this context), which she links with the narcissus and crocus, while

Calame (1998) 337-8 stresses the consequent links with mystery cult (Chapter 5, pp. 81-3).

22. Cf. Knox (1964) 155; Wallace (1979) 47; Markantonatos (2002) 205-7.

23. See also Markantonatos (2002) 186-7 and n. 23.

24. See Kirkwood (1986) 106; Mills (1997) 183-5.

25. See Chapter 7, pp. 26-8.

26. See Chapter 5, pp. 69-70.

27. See Hanson (1983) 120-2.

28. See Chapter 4, pp. 55-8, 62-3, for Oedipus' anger at his own thwarted ambition.

29. Cf. Carey (1986).

30. Cf. esp. Winnington-Ingram (1980) 339-40; Allison (1984); Blundell (1993); Krummen (1993); Jouanna (1995); Edmunds (1996); Markantonatos (2002) 179-220.

31. The verb here (*eustomeô*) can also mean 'avoid ill omen' and so 'to keep silent' (cf. Kamerbeek (1984) 27 for tragic examples), something particularly relevant to the Erinyes; cf. the chorus' description of the grove and their reluctance to speak in it (130-3), and their description of the rite (488-9).

32. *contra* Allison (1984); see Blundell (1993) 288-9.

33. For the details, see Chapter 3, p. 44 and n. 27.

34. Cf. Kirsten (1973) and Krummen (1993).

35. Jebb (1900) xxxvi-vii invokes the authority of Ister (third century BC), who, in describing the geography of Attica, uses the unaccompanied adjective as a noun ('the Brazen'), but the particular sentence ('from here to Colonus along (or 'past') the Brazen, as it is called') does not make it clear whether he is referring to a region or route ('along') or a specific place ('past').

36. See Chapter 3 n. 27; also Chapter 5, pp. 71-4.

37. See Chapter 5, pp. 81-2.

38. See esp. Segal (1981) ch. 11; Blundell (1993) 287-8.

39. See Budelmann (2000b).

40. See Chapter 7, pp. 114-15.

41. See Chapter 5, pp. 81-3.

42. See Krummen (1993) 212.

43. See Parker (1987); Krummen (1993) esp. 201-2. On the deme generally, see Osborne (1985).

44. Stockton (1990) 57-116 gives an account (and 19-56 for an historical narrative); on the religious side of Cleisthenes' actions, see Parker (1996) esp. ch. 7.

45. See Chapter 1, p. 10.

46. See, e.g., Knox (1964) 143; Flashar (2000) 164-5.

47. See Hanson (1983) esp. ch. 8; also Chapter 1, pp. 14-17; also (on the olive) Chapter 5, pp. 68-9.

48. See Gomme, Andrewes and Dover (1981) 167.

49. Krummen (1993) 216.

50. See Blundell (1993) 291f. and Mills (1997) 168-71.

51. See Mills (1997) 79-86.

52. Kirkwood (1986); cf. also Blundell (1993) 303.
53. Kirkwood (1986) 100 (my italics).
54. Blundell (1993) 300f. restricts divine support to the defence of Attica.
55. See Chapter 7, pp. 112-13.
56. See Cairns (1993) 222-3, 276-87.
57. Mills (1997) 185.

7. Characters

1. Cf. Easterling (1977); Gould (1978); Blundell (1989) 16-25; Easterling (1990); Goldhill (1990).
2. For other reversals, see Taplin (1971) 31-2.
3. See Edmunds (1996) 125-6; Blundell (1989) 228-9.
4. See Winnington-Ingram (1980) 274.
5. On his failings with regard to his daughters' livelihoods, see above, pp. 129-31.
6. See Blundell (1989) 230-2, 248-53; Mills (1997) 160-85; also Reinhardt (1979) 208 (= (1947) 216).
7. Though Theseus, like Heracles, was said to have both human (Aegeus) and divine (Poseidon) fathers, there is no explicit trace of this latter element in the *OC*; cf. Mills (1997) 176-7.
8. See Chapter 5, pp. 80-4.
9. See Mills (1997) 173.
10. Jebb (1900) ad loc., 164.
11. Blundell (1993) interprets this as a positive concern, signally lacking in Thebes, which keeps Athens safe; see also (cautiously) Avezzù and Guidorizzi (2008) ad 1031-2, 328-9.
12. See Taplin (1971) 31-2 for the many structural and thematic parallels between the scenes.
13. See Chapter 5, pp. 82-5.
14. In Euripides' *Heracles* (*c*. 415 BC), Theseus again appears to offer succour to a distressed and apparently broken hero (1153f.). But, in that play, when Heracles tries to draw back from touching him for fear of spreading his pollution, Theseus explicitly denies the possibility (1398-1400). Here in the *OC* he makes no such statement, so it is clear at least that pollution is a still a tremendous factor – and that the King is cautious as ever.
15. See Mills (1997) 170 n. 35.
16. For other possible allusions, see Chapter 5, pp. 81-2.
17. His awareness reminds one of the forbearance which Achilles shows towards Priam in the last book of the *Iliad* when the Trojan king attempts to refuse his hospitality (*Il*. 24.568-70).
18. *contra* Blundell (1989) 252.
19. See Easterling (1967) 1: 'so repellent a hypocrite that we are in no doubt that we are right to sympathize with Oedipus when he contemptuously rejects him'; Reinhardt (1979) 211 (= (1947) 219): 'repulsively hypocritical';

Segal (1981) 379: 'perverter of civilized values'; Blundell (1989) 232-8; Halliwell (1997) 138-40; Garvie (2005) 75: 'an unscrupulous villain'.

20. Blundell (1989) 237.

21. See, e.g., Adams (1957); Kirkwood (1986) 114: 'dishonestly hypocritical'; Markantonatos (2007) 153 (though more balanced at 104-7); *contra*, e.g., Winnington-Ingram (1980) 276: 'the poet has no intention to deprive him of sympathy or deny him all sincerity'; see also Easterling (1967); Burian (1974) 423-5; Blundell (1989) 238-48, esp. 247; Cairns (1993) 225-6.

22. See Winnington-Ingram (1980) 277, also Chapter 5, pp. 78-7.

23. See Sommerstein (1995-6).

24. See Easterling (1967); Winnington-Ingram (1980) 257, 276; also Chapter 4, pp. 62-3 for Oedipus' own ambition, the precise nature of the resentment revealed in this scene, and the 'sceptres and thrones' theme.

25. Easterling (1967) 5-6.

26. On this theme ('nursing'), see above, pp. 129-31.

27. See Burian (1974) 422-4.

28. See Blundell (1989) 245.

29. Blundell (1989) 242-3 argues that it highlights the essential difference between Theseus and Polyneices, and hence justifies Oedipus in rejecting his son's advances, for Polyneices' state is 'a just return for reducing his father to such straits'.

30. See Chapter 3, pp. 40-1.

31. Cf. Cairns (1993) 225-6.

32. For the significance of his relationship with these goddesses, see Chapter 5, pp. 71-4.

33. Cf. Burian (1974) 427.

34. On this contradiction, see Easterling (1999) 97.

35. We might remember that, even in the *OT* after the moment of his downfall, Oedipus was still an insistent and controlling figure, attempting to determine, over Creon's authority, what was to happen to him (*OT* 1435-45, 1516-23).

36. Kirkwood (1958) 245; Segal (1981) 398-9; Easterling (1999) interprets the 'short word' between Theseus and Oedipus as showing their sympathy (see also Easterling (2006c) 135).

37. For the messenger's variation (1615-16), see above, p. 130. For another example of repeated phrasing confined to Oedipus ('sceptres and thrones'), see Chapter 4, pp. 62-3.

38. See above, pp. 122-3.

39. Pat Easterling suggests to me that a gender neutral translation is preferable (i.e. 'reverend deities'), but the cult title *Semnai Theai* is so well associated with the Eumenides that an Athenian audience would surely make the link.

40. See Easterling (1999) on this speech and its many contradictions.

41. See Chapter 5, pp. 80-1 on this aspect of hero cult.

42. See Chapter 4, pp. 54, 58.

43. See Blundell (1989) 26-59, 226-59, esp. 253.

44. On the 'nursing' theme, see above, pp. 129-31.

45. See Blundell (1989) 234.

46. He later calls him 'most dear of hosts' (1552), while Antigone calls Theseus' men 'dearest' (1103); see above, pp. 108-9 for Antigone's notion of *philia*.

47. See above, pp. 125-6.

48. See MacDowell (1978) 92; Garland (1990) 256-7, 261-2.

49. See Winnington-Ingram (1980) 256.

50. See Halliwell (1997) 140.

51. *contra* Blundell (1989) 241.

52. See Chapter 4, pp. 63-4.

53. See Easterling (1967) 2-3.

54. Easterling (1967) 4-6, 12-13 interprets these themes more as a means of contrasting sons and daughters, rather than emphasising the way in which the reciprocities seem to tie all the members of the family in a particularly unsatisfying relationship. For an enormously detailed consideration of the *trophê* theme, see Daly (1986a), (1986b).

55. It is thus a part of his *kharis* scheme; see Chapter 5, pp. 82-3.

56. Sophocles may be recalling Herodotus' famous description of Egyptian gender roles (2.35); see Asheri, Lloyd and Corcella (2007) 262-3. Not only are the sons neglectful of their duty (bad enough), but it renders them the equivalents of foreigners!

57. Easterling (1999) 104-5 thinks the current circumstance 'a creative and transformative' example of the theme, but the *philia* here is far from positive. For Oedipus' problems in this regard, see above, pp. 126-7.

58. See MacDowell (1978) 84-6, 91.

59. This word has often seemed out of place, for there has been no 'ancient' promise from Theseus (and none really directed explicitly towards the daughters), and a variety of emendations proposed for it. But in this context, it would help to underline Oedipus' hurried attempt to make up for his lack of foresight in his daughters' future; see further Chapter 3, p. 47 and n. 39.

60. *contra* Blundell (1989) 246 and n. 63.

61. See, e.g., Easterling (1967), Markantonatos (2007) for more favourable views.

62. See Winnington-Ingram (1980) 257-60.

63. See Chapter 4, pp. 62-3 for other such moments.

64. See Winnington-Ingram (1980) 255; also Cairns (1993) 227.

65. Reinhardt (1979) 219 (= (1947) 228).

8. Oedipal Receptions

1. Three studies are indispensible for the reception of the *OC*: Flashar (1996); Markantonatos (2007) 231-55 and Rodighiero (2008); see also Morwood (2008) 83-119, esp. 115-18.

2. See Hall and Macintosh (2005) 12-14; Morwood (2008) 115-18.

3. See Goff and Simpson (1997) 192-3.

4. See Markantonatos (2007) 234-5; Holford-Strevens (1999) 229-30, 235-6, 239.

5. See Rodighiero (2008) 9-22; Edmunds (1976).
6. Accessed at http://www.apgrd.ox.ac.uk.
7. APGRD ID 8447; Hall and Macintosh (2005) 183-214; Markantonatos (2007) 236-8.
8. Macintosh (1997) 318-19; APGRD ID 15.
9. APGRD ID 861.
10. APGRD ID 6699.
11. See, e.g., Hester (1984) 21-3, March (1987) 148-54 and Müller (1996); also Chapter 1, p. 15 and n. 29 for the *OC*'s date.
12. APGRD ID 310.
13. APGRD ID 1417 (also 1477 for reperformance).
14. APGRD ID 5599.
15. APGRD ID 9447; cf. http://www.studiooyunculari.com/default.asp?2,4,8.
16. APGRD ID 5988.
17. See Mattietti (2005) (not Vlad (2005), as APGRD have it).
18. APGRD ID 2225 (also 2226-8 for reperformances); Rodighiero (2008) 33-6; (text) Tosti-Croce (2001) 1-60 (French) and 61-132 (Italian).
19. APGRD ID 8360; Rodighiero (2008) 37-8; (text) Tosti-Croce (2001) 133-86.
20. APGRD ID 2239; (text) Tosti-Croce (2001) 299-528; Markantonatos (2007) 240.
21. APGRD ID 2240 (also 2241, 2242, 6845, 2151 for reperformances); cf. Flashar (1991) 80-1.
22. APGRD ID 2182; see Rodighiero (2008) 52-4.
23. APGRD ID 5804.
24. See the criticisms advanced by Linforth (1951) and Bernard (2001).
25. Burian (1997b) 281; APGRD ID 1765 (also 2049, 5462, 4475 for reperformances); (text) Breuer (1989); Rodighiero (2008) 67-74; Goff and Simpson (2007) 178-218.

Further Reading

This guide to further reading limits itself to what is most useful, in the author's opinion, of the works cited in the bibliography. The scholarship on Greek tragedy is enormous, but reliable introductions are afforded by the companion volumes edited by Easterling (1997) and Allan and Storey (2004), while Csapo and Slater (1995) present and translate many of the ancient documents fundamental for an understanding of Athenian theatre.

The text of the poet used in this volume is that of Lloyd-Jones and Wilson (Oxford 1990a), with some of their decisions – and reactions to reviews – explained in (1990b) and (1997) (for differences adopted in this book, see the *Critical Appendix* at the end of this section); the edition of Dawe (1996) has a useful metrical appendix, as does that of Avezzù and Guidorizzi (2008). Sophocles' *testimonia* and fragments are collected by Radt (1999), supplemented with Pearson (1917). Of translations, that facing the text in Jebb's commentary (see below) is still useful (if a trifle archaic), the Loeb by Lloyd-Jones (1994) is helpfully literal and blessed with a very useful introduction; Fitzgerald (1959) is highly readable, though he sometimes augments the Greek (e.g. the phrase 'the flash of Zeus' (95) is rendered as 'God's smiling lightning'), Watling's older Penguin (1947) has been superseded by the much more nuanced Fagles (1984), while the recent collaboration of Grennan and Kitzinger (2005) seeks, more than most and with overall success, to reproduce the theatrical immediacy of Sophocles' language in a variety of ways, including vivid stage directions rather than the somewhat formulaic 'alas'! *vel sim.* For a very complete list of translations, cf. Markantonatos (2007) 265-6; also Classe (2000) 1311-14.

The best English-language commentary on this play is still that by Sir Richard Jebb (1900), the utility of which is pointed out by Rehm (2004) in his introduction to its reissue. Kamerbeek (1984) contains much of value (certainly more than that expressed by Lloyd-Jones in his reviews of the series), as do the copious notes of Avezzù and Guidorizzi (2008), though we await eagerly the forthcoming commentary by Pat Easterling, excerpts from which she was kind enough to show me.

There are many individual studies of Sophocles, among which Blundell (1989), Budelmann (2000a), Knox (1964), Reinhardt (1979), Taplin (1983) and Winnington-Ingram (1980) may be recommended, while the briefer volumes of Garvie (2005) and Morwood (2008) are extremely useful starting points (and Flashar (2000) for German readers).

On the *OC* itself, Markantonatos (2007) is very helpful in its coverage of the major issues – as is the second half of Edmunds (1996) – and it has an extremely complete bibliography, while (for the German reader) Bernard (2001) is always stimulating, if sometimes a trifle iconoclastic. Though concerned mostly with the matter of religion (on which issue in general, Parker (1999) is essential), Linforth (1951) is still worth reading. The individual chapters in the general works of Blundell (1989), Reinhardt (1979) and Winnington-Ingram (1980) are essential to an informed reading of the play.

Of more specialised studies, Burian (1974) is very good on suppliancy, as is Blundell (1993) on the ideal of Athens, Calame (1998) on mystery cult, and Wallace (1979) on hero cult (cf. also Seaford (1994a) for a general approach); Easterling (2006c) is challenging on the details (or lack thereof) surrounding Oedipus' death; Krummen (1993) puts the depiction of the landscape into a broader historical framework, and Rosenmeyer (1952) is refreshingly trenchant on Oedipus' character.

CRITICAL APPENDIX
(Divergences from the OCT)

Chapter 4, p. 55 and n. 11 (*OC* 521, 544, 547-8)
Chapter 5, p. 69 and n. 8 (716)
Chapter 5, p. 74 and n. 36 (1653 & 1655)
Chapter 5, p. 75 and n. 39 (487)
Chapter 5, p. 83 and n. 72 (1752)
Chapter 7, p. 112 (1640)

Bibliography

Adams, S. (1957), *Sophocles the Playwright*, Toronto.

Allan, A. & Storey, I. (2004), *A Guide to Ancient Greek Drama*, Oxford.

Allan, W. (2001a), 'Euripides in Megale Hellas: some aspects of the early reception of tragedy', *G&R* 48: 67-86.

Allan, W. (2001b), *Euripides: Children of Heracles*, Warminster.

Allan, W. (2006), 'Divine Justice and Cosmic Order in Early Greek Epic', *JHS* 126: 1-35.

Allan, W. (2008), *Euripides: Helen*, Cambridge.

Allison, R. (1984), ' "This is the place": why is Oidipous at Colonus?', *Prudentia* 16: 67-91.

Arnott, P. (1962), *Greek Scenic Conventions in the Fifth Century BC*, Oxford.

Asheri, D., Lloyd, A. & Corcella, A. (2007), *A Commentary on Herodotus Books I-IV* (Murray, O. & Moreno, A. (eds)), Oxford.

Avezzù, G. & Guidorizzi, G. (2008), *Sofocle: Edipo a Colono*, Rome.

Baldry, H.C. (1956), 'The dramatization of the Theban legend', *G&R* 3: 24-57.

Bernabé, A. (1987), *Poetae Epici Graeci: Pars I*, Stuttgart.

Bernard, W. (2001), *Das Ende des Ödipus bei Sophokles: Untersuchung zur Interpretation des 'Ödipus auf Kolonos'*, Munich.

Blundell, M.W. (1989), *Helping Friends and Harming Enemies: A Study in Sophocles and Greek Ethics*, Cambridge.

Blundell, M.W. (1993), 'The ideal of Athens in Oedipus at Colonus', in Sommerstein et al. (1993): 287-306.

Bowie, A. (1997), 'Tragic filters for history: Euripides' *Supplices* and Sophocles' *Philoctetes*', in Pelling (1997a).

Breuer, L. (1989), *The Gospel at Colonus*, New York.

Budelmann, F. (2000a), *The Language of Sophocles*, Cambridge.

Budelmann, F. (2000b), 'Visual and verbal symbolism in Greek tragedy: the case of the uncut rock in Oedipus at Colonus', in Hardwick, L., Easterling, P., Ireland, S., Lowe, N. & Macintosh, F. (eds), *Theatre: Ancient and Modern*, Milton Keynes (www2.open.ac. uk/ ClassicalStudies/GreekPlays/Conf99/index.htm).

Burian, P. (1974), 'Suppliant and saviour: Oedipus at Colonus', *Phoenix* 28: 408-29.

Burian, P. (1997a), 'Myth into *muthos*: the shaping of tragic plot', in Easterling (1997): 178-208.

Burian (1997b), 'Tragedy adapted for stages and screens: the Renaissance to the present', in Easterling (1997): 228-83.

Burkert, W. (1985), 'Opferritual bei Sophokles. Pragmatik – Symbolik –

Bibliography

Theater', *AU* 28: 5-20 (also in Rösler, W. (ed.) (2007), *Walter Burkert: Kleine Schriften VII: Tragica et Historica*, Göttingen: 73-91).

Burkert, W. (1987), *Ancient Mystery Cults*, Cambridge MA.

Burton, R.W.B. (1980), *The Chorus in Sophocles' Tragedies*, Oxford.

Bushnell, R. (1988), *Prophesying Tragedy: Sign and Voice in Sophocles' Theban Tragedies*, Ithaca.

Cairns, D. (1993), *Aidos: the Psychology and Ethics of Honour and Shame in Ancient Greek Literature*, Oxford.

Calame, C. (1998), 'Mort héroique et culte à mystére dans *l'Oedipe à Colone* de Sophocle', in Graf, F. (ed.), *Ansichten griechischer Rituale. Geburtstags-Symposium für Walter Burkert*, Stuttgart: 326-56.

Calder, W.M. (1971), 'Sophoclean Apologia: *Philoctetes*' *GRBS* 12: 153-74.

Calder, W.M. (1985), 'The political and literary sources of Sophocles' *Oedipus Coloneus*', in Calder, W.M., Goldsmith, U. & Kenevan, P. (eds), *Hypatia: Essays in Classics, Comparative Literature and Philosophy presented to Hazel Barnes on her Seventieth Birthday*, Boulder: 1-14.

Campbell, L. (1879), *Sophocles: The Plays and Fragments*, vol. 1, Oxford.

Campbell, L. (1891), *A Guide to Greek Tragedy for English Readers*, London.

Carey, C. (1986), 'The second stasimon of the *Oedipus Tyrannus*', *JHS* 106: 175-9.

Classe, O. (2000), *The Encyclopedia of Literary Translation into English*, London.

Clinton, K. (1992), *Myth and Cult: The Iconography of the Eleusinian Mysteries*, Stockholm.

Cohen, D. (1991), *Law, Sexuality and Society: The Enforcement of Morals in Classical Athens*, Cambridge.

Colchester, L.S. (1942), 'Justice and Death in Sophocles', *CQ* 36: 21-8.

Collard, C. (1975), *Euripides: Supplices* (2 vols), Groningen.

Collard, C. (2005), 'Euripidean fragmentary plays', in McHardy, F., Robson, J. & Harvey, D. (eds), *Lost Dramas of Classical Athens: Greek Tragic Fragments*, Exeter: 49-62.

Connolly, A. (1998), 'Was Sophocles heroised as Dexion?', *JHS* 118: 1-21.

Croally, N. (1994), *Euripidean Polemic*, Cambridge.

Csapo, E. (2007), 'The men who built the theatres', in Wilson (2007): 87-121 (with appendix by Goette, H.).

Csapo, E. & Slater, W.J. (1995), *The Context of Ancient Drama*, Ann Arbor.

Currie, B.G.F. (2005), *Pindar and the Cult of Heroes*, Oxford.

D'Angour, A. (1997), 'How the dithyramb got its shape', *CQ* 47: 331-351.

Daly, J. (1986a), '*Oedipus Coloneus*: Sophocles' *Threpteria* to Athens I', *QUCC* 22: 75-93.

Daly, J. (1986b), '*Oedipus Coloneus*: Sophocles' *Threpteria* to Athens II', *QUCC* 23: 65-84.

Davidson, J.F. (1986), 'The Sophoclean battleground', *Eranos* 84: 107-17.

Davies, M. (1982), 'The end of Sophocles' *Oedipus Tyrannus*', *Hermes* 110: 268-77.

Dawe, R.D. (1996), *Sophocles: Oedipus Coloneus*, 3rd edn, Leipzig.

161

Bibliography

Dawe, R.D. (2006), *Sophocles: Oedipus Rex*, 2nd edn, Cambridge.

Dover, K.J. (1993), *Aristophanes Frogs*, Oxford.

Dunn, F. (1992), 'Introduction: beginning at Colonus', *YCS* 29: 1-12.

Dunn, F. (1996), *Tragedy's End: Closure and Innovation in Euripidean Drama*, New York.

Easterling, P. (1967), 'Oedipus and Polynices', *PCPS* 13: 1-13.

Easterling, P. (1977), 'Character in Sophocles', *G&R* 24: 121-9.

Easterling, P. (1990), 'Constructing character in Greek tragedy' in Pelling, C. (ed.), *Characterization and Individuality in Greek Literature*, Oxford: 83-99.

Easterling, P. (ed.) (1997), *The Cambridge Companion to Greek Tragedy*, Cambridge.

Easterling, P. (1999), 'Plain words in Sophocles', in Griffin (1999): 95-107.

Easterling, P. (2006a), 'Sophocles – the first thousand years', in Davidson, J., Muecke, F. & Wilson, P. (eds), *Greek Drama III: Essays in Honour of Kevin Lee*, London: 1-15.

Easterling, P. (2006b), 'The image of the *polis* in Greek tragedy', in Hansen, M. (ed.), *The Imaginary Polis (Acts of the Copenhagen Polis Center 7)*: 49-91.

Easterling, P. (2006c), 'The death of Oedipus and what happened next', in Cairns, D. & Liapis, V. (eds), *Dionysalexandros: Essays on Aeschylus and his Fellow Tragedians in Honour of Alexander F. Garvie*, Swansea: 133-50.

Easterling, P. & Hall, E. (eds) (2002), *Greek and Roman Actors: Aspects of an Ancient Profession*, Cambridge.

Edmunds, L. (1976), 'Oedipus in the Middle Ages', *Antike und Abendland* XXII: 140-55.

Edmunds, L. (1981), 'The cults and the legend of Oedipus', *HSCP* 8: 221-38.

Edmunds, L. (1996), *Theatrical Space and Historical Space in Sophocles' Oedipus at Colonus*, Lanham.

Erp Taalman Kip, A.M. van (1987), 'Euripides and Melos', *Mnemosyne* 40: 414-19.

Esposito, S. (1996), 'The changing roles of the Sophoclean chorus', *Arion* 4: 85-114.

Euben, J.P. (1986), 'Political corruption in Euripides' *Orestes*', in Euben (ed.), *Greek Tragedy and Political Theory*, Berkeley: 222-51.

Eucken, C. (1979), 'Das anonyme Theseus-drama und der Ödipus auf Kolonos', *MH* 36: 136-41.

Farnell, L.R. (1921), *Greek Hero Cults and Ideas of Immortality*, Oxford.

Finglass, P.J. (2009), 'The end of Sophocles' *Oedipus Rex*', *Philologus* 153: 42-62.

Finkelberg, M. (2002), 'Religion and biography in Sophocles' *Oedipus at Colonus*', in Shulman, D. & Stroumsa, G. (eds), *Self and Self-Transformation in the History of Religions*, Oxford: 173-82.

Finkelberg, M. (1997), 'Oedipus' apology and Sophoclean criticism', *Mnemosyne* 50: 561-76.

Bibliography

Fitzgerald, R. (1959), 'Oedipus at Colonus', in Grene, D. & Lattimore, R. (eds), *The Complete Greek Tragedies, vol. II: Sophocles*, Chicago: 79-155.

Flashar, H. (1991), *Inszenierung der Antike: das griechische Drama auf der Bühne der Neuzeit 1585-1990*, Munich.

Flashar, H. (1996), 'Vorstufen und Wirkungsgeschichte', in Flashar, H. & Schadewaldt, W., *Sophokles, Ödipus auf Kolonos*, Frankfurt: 119-38.

Flashar, H. (2000), *Sophokles. Dichter im demokratischen Athen*, Munich.

Fraenkel, E. (1950), *Aeschylus Agamemnon* (3 vols), Oxford.

Friedrich, R. (1996), 'Everything to do with Dionysus?', in Silk (1996): 257-83.

Gagarin, M. (2002), *Antiphon the Athenian*, Austin.

Gardiner, C. (1987), *The Sophoclean Chorus: A Study of Character and Function*, Iowa.

Garland, R. (1985), *The Greek Way of Death*, London.

Garvie, A.E. (2005), *The Plays of Sophocles*, London.

Goff, B. & Simpson, M. (2007), *Crossroads in the Black Aegean: Oedipus, Antigone and Dramas of the African Diaspora*, Oxford.

Goldhill, S. (1987), 'The Great Dionysia and civic ideology', *JHS* 107: 58-76 (also in Winkler & Zeitlin (1990): 97-129).

Goldhill, S. (1990), 'Character and action, representation and reading Greek tragedy and its critics', in Pelling, C. (ed.), *Characterization and Individuality in Greek Literature*, Oxford: 100-27.

Gomme, A.W., Andrewes, A. & Dover, K.J. (1981), *An Historical Commentary on Thucydides Volume V: Book VIII*, Oxford.

Gould, J. (1974) 'Hiketeia', *JHS* 93: 74-103 (also in Gould, J. (2001), *Myth, Ritual, Memory and Exchange: Essays in Greek Literature and Culture*, Oxford: 22-77).

Gould, J. (1978), 'Dramatic character and "human intelligibility" in Greek tragedy', *PCPS* 204: 43-67 (also in Gould, J. (2001), *Myth, Ritual, Memory and Exchange: Essays in Greek Literature and Culture*, Oxford: 78-111).

Grennan, E. & Kitzinger, R. (2005), *Sophocles: Oedipus at Colonus*, Oxford.

Griffin, J. (1998), 'The social function of Attic tragedy', *CQ* 48: 39-61.

Griffin, J. (1999), *Sophocles Revisited: Essays Presented to Sir Hugh Lloyd-Jones*, Oxford.

Griffith, M. (1999), *Sophocles Antigone*, Cambridge.

Hägg, R. (1987), 'Gifts to the heroes', in Linders, T. & Nordquist, G. (eds), *Gifts to the Gods: Proceedings of the Uppsala Symposium 1985*, Uppsala: 93-9.

Hall, E. & Macintosh, F. (2005), *Greek Tragedy and the British Theatre 1660-1914*, Oxford.

Halliwell, S. (1982), 'Notes on some Aristophanic jokes', *LCM* 7: 153-4.

Halliwell, S. (1997) 'Between public and private: tragedy and the Athenian experience of rhetoric', in Pelling (1997a).

Hanson, V.D. (1983), *Warfare and Agriculture in Classical Greece*, Pisa.

Harrison, A.R.W. (1968), *The Law of Athens: The Family and Property*, Oxford.

Bibliography

Harrison, A.R.W. (1971), *The Law of Athens: Procedure*, Oxford.
Harrison, S.J. (1989), 'Sophocles and the cult of Philoctetes', *JHS* 109: 173-5.
Heath, M. (1987a), *The Poetics of Greek Tragedy*, London.
Heath, M. (1987b), *Political Comedy in Aristophanes*, Göttingen.
Heath, M. (1997), 'Aristophanes and the discourse of politics', in Dobrov, G. (ed.), *The City as Comedy*, Chapel Hill: 230-49.
Heiden, B. (1993), 'Emotion, acting and the Athenian *ethos*', in Sommerstein et al. (1993): 145-66.
Henrichs, A. (1983), 'The "sobriety" of Oedipus: Sophocles *OC* 100 misunderstood', *HSCP* 87: 87-100.
Henrichs, A. (1994), 'Anonymity and polarity: unknown gods and nameless altars at the Areopagos', *ICS* 19: 27-58.
Herington, J. (1985), *Poetry into Drama*, Berkeley.
Hester, D.A. (1984), 'The banishment of Oedipus; a neglected theory on the end of the *Oedipus Rex*', *Antichthon* 18: 13-23.
Holford-Strevens, L. (1999), 'Sophocles in Rome', in Griffin (1999): 219-59.
Hornblower, S. (2008), *A Commentary on Thucydides Vol. III: Books 5.25–8.109*, Oxford.
Hutchinson, G.O. (1985), *Aeschylus: Septem contra Thebas*, Oxford.
Jameson, M. (1971), 'Sophocles and the Four Hundred', *Historia* 20: 541-68.
Jebb, R.C. (1900), *Sophocles: The Plays and Fragments Part II: the Oedipus Coloneus* (3rd edn), Cambridge.
Jebb, R. C. (1902), *Sophocles: the Plays and Fragments Part I: the Oedipus Tyrannus* (3rd edn), Cambridge.
Jones, J. (1962), *On Aristotle and Greek Tragedy*, London.
Jouanna, J. (1995), 'Espaces sacrés, rites et oracles', *REG* 108: 38-58.
Just, R. (1989), *Women in Athenian Law and Life*, London.
Kamerbeek, J. (1967), *The Plays of Sophocles Part IV: The Oedipus Tyrannus*, Leiden.
Kamerbeek, J. (1984), *The Plays of Sophocles Part VII: The Oedipus Coloneus*, Leiden.
Kannicht, R. (2004), *Tragicorum Graecorum Fragmenta Volumen V: Euripides*, Göttingen.
Kearns, E. (1989), *The Heroes of Attica*, London.
Kelly, A. (2007), 'Stesikhoros and Helen', *MH* 64: 1-21.
Kirkwood, G. (1958), *A Study of Sophoclean Drama*, Ithaca.
Kirkwood, G. (1986), 'From Melos to Colonus: ... τίνας χώρους ἀφίγμεθ';' *TAPA* 116: 99-117.
Kirsten, E. (1973), 'Ur-Athen und die Heimat des Sophokles', *WS* 7: 5-26.
Knox, B.M.W. (1964), *The Heroic Temper: Studies in Sophoclean Tragedy*, Berkeley.
Kowalzig, B. (2007), *Singing for the Gods: Performances of Myth and Ritual in Archaic and Classical Greece*, Oxford.
Krummen, E. (1993), 'Athens and Attica: *polis* and countryside in Greek tragedy', in Sommerstein et al. (1993): 191-217.
Lardinois, A. (1992), 'Greek myths for Athenian rituals; religion and

politics in Aeschylus' *Eumenides* and Sophocles' *Oedipus Coloneus*', *GRBS* 33: 313-28.

Lefkowitz, M. (1978), 'The poet as hero: fifth-century autobiography and subsequent biographical fiction', *CQ* 28: 459-69.

Lefkowitz, M. (1981), *The Lives of the Greek Poets*, Baltimore.

Lefkowitz, M. (1991), *First Person Fictions: Pindar's Poetic 'I'*, Oxford.

Linforth, I.M. (1951), *Religion and Drama in 'Oedipus at Colonus'; University of California Publications in Classical Philology* 14: 74-192.

Lloyd-Jones, H. (1994), *Sophocles II*, Cambridge MA.

Lloyd-Jones, H. (2002), 'Curses and divine anger in early Greek epic: the Pisander scholion', *CQ* 52: 1-14.

Lloyd-Jones, H. & Wilson, N. (1990a), *Sophocles*, Oxford.

Lloyd-Jones, H. & Wilson, N. (1990b), *Sophoclea: Studies on the Text of Sophocles*, Oxford.

Lloyd-Jones, H. & Wilson, N. (1997), *Sophocles: Second Thoughts*, Göttingen.

Long, A.A. (1968), *Language and Thought in Sophocles*, London.

MacDowell, D.M. (1963), *Athenian Homicide Law in the Age of the Orators*, Manchester.

MacDowell, D.M. (1978), *The Law in Classical Athens*, Ithaca.

Macintosh, F. (1997), 'Tragedy in performance: nineteenth- and twentieth-century productions', in Easterling (1997): 284-323.

March, J. (1987), *The Creative Poet*, London.

Markantonatos, A. (2002), *Tragic Narrative: A Narratological Study of Sophocles' Oedipus at Colonus*, Berlin.

Markantonatos, A. (2007), *Oedipus at Colonus. Sophocles, Athens, and the World*, Berlin.

Mastronarde, D. (1994), *Euripides: Phoinissai*, Cambridge.

McDevitt, A.S. (1972), 'The nightingale and the olive: remarks on the first stasimon of *Oedipus Coloneus*', in Hanslik, R., Lesky, A. & Schwabl, H. (eds), *Antidosis: Festschrift für Walther Kraus zum 70. Geburtstag*, Vienna: 227-37.

Michaelides, S. (1978), *The Music of Ancient Greece: An Encyclopedia*, London.

Mills, S. (1997), *Theseus, Tragedy and the Athenian Empire*, Oxford.

Minadeo, R. (1994), *The Thematic Sophocles*, Amsterdam.

Morwood, J. (2008), *The Tragedies of Sophocles*, Exeter.

Müller, C.W. (1984), *Zur Datierung des sophokleischen Ödipus*, Wiesbaden.

Müller, C.W. (1996), 'Die thebanische Trilogie des Sophokles und Ihre Aufführung im Jahre 401. Zur Frühgeschichte der antiken Sophoklesrezeption und der Überlieferung des Textest', *RM* 139: 193-224 (also in Müller, C.W. (1999), *Kleine Schriften zur antiken Literatur und Geistesgeschichte*, Leipzig: 215-48).

Mueller-Goldingen, C. (1985), *Untersuchungen zu den Phoinissen des Euripides*, Stuttgart.

Bibliography

Murray, P. & Wilson, P. (eds) (2004), *Music and the Muses: The Culture of Mousike in the Classical Athenian City*, Oxford.

O'Connell, M.J. (1967), '*Antigone* and the Oedipus plays as unified', *Classical Bulletin* 44: 22-3, 25.

Olson, S.D. (1998), *Aristophanes Peace*, Oxford.

Osborne, R. (1985), *Demos: The Discovery of Classical Attica*, Cambridge.

Osborne, R. (1993), 'Competitive festivals and the *polis*: a context for dramatic festivals at Athens', in Sommerstein et al. (1993): 21-37.

Ostwald, M. (1986), *From Popular Sovereignty to the Sovereignty of Law: Law, Society and Politics in Fifth-century Athens*, Berkeley.

Parker, R. (1983), *Miasma: Pollution and Purification in early Greek Religion*, Oxford.

Parker, R. (1987), 'Festivals of the Attic demes', in Linders, T. & Nordquist, G. (eds), *Gifts to the Gods: Proceedings of the Uppsala Symposium 1985*, Uppsala: 137-47.

Parker, R. (1996), *Athenian Religion: A History*, Oxford.

Parker, R. (1999), 'Through a glass darkly: Sophocles and the divine', in Griffin (1999): 11-30.

Parsons, P. (1977), 'The Lille "Stesichorus"', *ZPE* 26: 7-36.

Pearson, A.C. (1917), *Sophocles Fragments*, Cambridge.

Pelling, C. (ed.) (1997a), *Greek Tragedy and the Historian*, Oxford.

Pelling, C. (1997b), 'Conclusion', in Pelling (1997a): 213-35.

Phillips, D. *Avengers of Blood: Homicide in Athenian Law and Custom from Draco to Demosthenes*, Stuttgart 2008.

Pickard-Cambridge, A.W. (1946), *The Theatre of Dionysus in Athens*, Oxford.

Pickard-Cambridge, A. (1962), *Dithyramb, Tragedy and Comedy* (2nd edn rev. by Webster, T.B.L.), Oxford.

Pickard-Cambridge, A.W. (1968), *The Dramatic Festivals of Athens* (2nd edn rev. by Gould, J. & Lewis, D.M.), Oxford.

Podlecki, A. J. (1966), *The Political Background of Aeschylean Tragedy*, Michigan.

Radt, S. (ed.) (1985), *Tragicorum Graecorum Fragmenta*, vol. III: *Aeschylus*, Göttingen.

Radt, S. (ed.) (1999), *Tragicorum Graecorum Fragmenta*, vol. IV: *Sophocles* (corr. edn), Göttingen.

Rehm , R. (1992), *Greek Tragic Theatre*, London.

Rehm, R. (2002), *The Play of Space: Spatial Transformations in Greek Tragedy*, Princeton.

Rehm, R. (2004), 'Introduction', in Jebb, R.C., *Sophocles Plays: Oedipus Coloneus*, London: 31-56.

Reinhardt, K. (1979), *Sophocles*, Oxford (tr. by Harvey, D. & H.; original Frankfurt am Main, 1947).

Rhodes, P.J. (2006), *A History of the Classical Greek World*, Oxford.

Richardson, N.J. (1974), *The Homeric Hymn to Demeter*, Oxford.

Robert, C. (1915) *Oidipus: Geschichte eines poetischen Stoffs im griechischen Altertum* (2 vols), Berlin.

Bibliography

Rodighiero, A. (2007), *Una serata a Colono: Fortuna del secondo Edipo*, Florence.

Rosenbloom, D. (1993), 'Phrynichos' *Capture of Miletus*', *Philologus* 137: 159-96.

Rosenmeyer, T (1952), 'The wrath of Oedipus', *Phoenix* 6: 92-112.

Rosenmeyer, T. (1993), 'Elusory voices: thoughts about the Sophoclean chorus', in Rosen, R. & Farrell, J. (eds), *Nomodeiktes: Greek Studies in Honour of Martin Ostwald*, Ann Arbor: 557-71.

Schunk, L. (1907), *Sophokles' Oedipus auf Kolonos*, Münster.

Scott, W.C. (1996), *Musical Design in Sophoclean Theater*, Hanover.

Scullion, S. (1994), *Three Studies in Athenian Dramaturgy*, Stuttgart.

Scullion, S. (1999), 'Tradition and invention in Eurpidean aitiology', in Cropp, M., Lee, K. & Sansone, D. (eds), *Euripides and the Tragic Theatre in the Late Fifth Century* (*ICS* 24-5 [1999-2000]), Illinois: 217-34.

Scullion, S. (2002a), 'Tragic dates' *CQ* 52: 81-101.

Scullion, S. (2002b), ' "Nothing to do with Dionysus": tragedy misconceived as ritual', *CQ* 52: 102-37.

Seaford, R. (1994a), *Reciprocity and Ritual*, Oxford.

Seaford, R. (1994b), 'Sophokles and the mysteries', *Hermes* 122: 275-88.

Seaford, R. (1996), 'Something to do with Dionysus – tragedy and the Dionysiac: a response to Rainer Friedrich', in Silk (1996): 284-94.

Seaford, R. (2000), 'The social function of Attic tragedy: a response to Jasper Griffin', *CQ* 50: 30-44.

Seale, D. (1982), *Vision and Stagecraft in Sophocles*, Melbourne.

Segal, C. (1981), *Tragedy and Civilization*, Cambridge MA.

Segal, C. (2001), *Oedipus Tyrannus: Tragic Heroism and the Limits of Knowledge* (2nd edn), Oxford.

Seidensticker, B. (1972), 'Beziehungen zwischen den beiden Oidipusdramen des Sophokles', *Hermes* 100: 255-74 (also in Holzhausen, J. (ed.) (2005), *Über das Vergnügen an tragischen Gegenständen: Studien zum antiken Drama*, Leipzig: 1-28).

Sewell-Rutter, N. (2007), *Guilt by Descent: Moral Inheritance and Decision-making in Greek Tragedy*, Oxford.

Silk, M. (ed.) (1996), *Tragedy and the Tragic: Greek Theatre and Beyond*, Oxford.

Shields, M. (1961), 'Sight and blindness imagery in the *Oedipus Coloneus*', *Phoenix* 15: 63-73.

Siewert, P. (1979), 'Poseidon Hippios am Kolonos und die athenischen Hippeis', in Bowersock, G., Burkert, W. & Putnam, M. (eds), *Arktouros: Hellenic Studies Presented to B.M.W. Knox on the Occasion of his 65th Birthday*, Berlin: 280-9.

Singh Dugha, U. (2005), 'Choral identity in Sophocles' *Oedipus Coloneus*', *AJP* 126: 333-62.

Sinn, U. (1993), 'Greek sanctuaries as places of refuge', in Marinatos, N. & Hägg, R. (eds), *Greek Sanctuaries: New Approaches* (London): 88-109.

Snell, B. (1986), *Tragicorum Graecorum Fragmenta*, vol. I: *Didascaliae*

Bibliography

Tragicae, Catalogi Tragicorum et Tragoediarum, Testimonia et Fragmenta Tragicorum Minorum (corr. edn by R. Kannicht), Göttingen.

Sommerstein, A.H. (1985), *Aristophanes Peace*, Warminster.

Sommerstein, A.H. (1996), *Aristophanes Frogs*, Warminster.

Sommerstein, A.H. (1995-6), 'The seniority of Polyneikes in Aeschylus' *Septem*', *Museum Criticum* 30/31: 105-10.

Sommerstein, A.H. (1997) 'The theatre audience, the *demos*, and the *Suppliants* of Aeschylus', in Pelling (1997a): 63-80.

Sommerstein, A.H., Halliwell, S., Henderson, J. & Zimmermann, B. (eds) (1993), *Tragedy, Comedy and the Polis*, Bari.

Sourvinou-Inwood, C. (1995), *'Reading' Greek Death*, Oxford.

Sourvinou-Inwood, C. (2003), *Tragedy and Athenian Religion*, Lanham.

Spence, I.G. (1993), *The Cavalry of Classical Greece: a Social and Military History*, Oxford.

Stinton, T.W.C. (1976), 'The riddle at Colonus', *GRBS* 17: 323-8 (also in Stinton, T.W.C. (1990), *Collected Papers on Greek Tragedy*, Oxford: 265-70).

Stockton, D. (1990), *The Classical Athenian Democracy*, Oxford.

Suksi, A. (2001), 'The poet at Colonus: nightingales in Sophocles', *Mnemosyne* 54: 646-58.

Taplin, O. (1971), 'Significant actions in Sophocles' *Philoctetes*', *GRBS* 12: 25-44.

Taplin, O. (1977), *The Stagecraft of Aeschyus*, Oxford.

Taplin, O. (1980), *Greek Tragedy in Action*, London.

Taplin, O. (1983), 'Sophocles in his theatre', in de Romilly, J. (ed.), *Sophocle*, Geneva: 155-74.

Taplin, O. (1985), 'Lyric dialogue and dramatic construction in later Sophocles', *Dioniso* 55: 115-22.

Taplin, O. (1999), 'Spreading the word through Performance', in Goldhill, S. & Osborne, R. (eds), *Performance Culture and Athenian Democracy*, Cambridge: 33-57.

Torrance, R.M. (1965), 'Sophocles: some bearings', *HSCP* 69: 269-327.

Tosti-Croce, M. (ed.) (2001), *Edipo Coloneo*, Pesaro.

Travis, R. (1999), *Allegory and the Tragic Chorus in Sophocles' Oedipus at Colonus*, Lanham.

Vickers, M. (2008), *Sophocles and Alcibiades: Athenian Politics in Ancient Greek Literature*, Oxford.

Vidal-Naquet, P. (1980), 'Oedipus between two cities: an essay on *Oedipus at Colonus*', in Vernant, J.-P. & Vidal-Naquet, P., *Myth and Tragedy in Ancient Greece*, New York: 329-59.

Mattietti, G. (2005), 'Edipo in palcoscenico: quattro secoli di rivisitazioni letterarie e musicali', http://www.radio.rai.it/radio3/radio3_suite/archivio_2005/eventi/2005_01_12_oedipe/presentazione.pdf: 17-26.

Waldock, A.J.A. (1951), *Sophocles the Dramatist*, Cambridge.

Wallace, N. (1979), '*Oedipus at Colonus*: the hero in his collective context', *QUCC* 3: 39-52.

Webster, T.B.L. (1936), *Sophocles*, Oxford.

Bibliography

West, M.L. (1978), *Hesiod: Works and Days*, Oxford.

West, M.L. (1989), 'The early chronology of Attic tragedy', *CQ* 39: 251-4.

West, M.L. (1999), 'Ancestral curses', in Griffin (1999): 31-46.

Wilamowitz-Moellendorff, U. von (1917), 'Oedipus auf Kolonos', in Wilamowitz-Moellendorff, T. von, *Die dramatische Technik des Sophokles*, Berlin: 313-73.

Wiles, D. (1997), *Tragedy in Athens*, Cambridge.

Wiles, D. (2000), *Greek Theatre Performance: An Introduction*, Cambridge.

Wilson, J. (1997), *The Hero and the City: An Interpretation of Sophocles' Oedipus at Colonus*, Ann Arbor.

Wilson, P. (ed.) (2007), *The Greek Theatre and Festivals*, Oxford.

Wilson, P. (2008), 'Costing the *Dionysia*', in Revermann, M. & Wilson, P. (eds), *Performance, Reception, Iconography: Studies in Honour of Oliver Taplin*, Oxford: 88-127.

Winkler, J. & Zeitlin, F. (eds) (1990), *Nothing to Do with Dionysus? Attic Drama in its Social Context*, Princeton.

Winnington-Ingram, R.P. (1980), *Sophocles: An Interpretation*, Cambridge.

Woodbury, L. (1970), 'Sophocles among the generals', *Phoenix* 24: 209-24.

Zak, W. (1995), *The Polis and the Divine Order: The Oresteia, Sophocles and the Defence of Democracy*, Lewisburg.

Zeitlin, F. (1990), 'Thebes: theater of self and society in Athenian drama', in Winkler & Zeitlin (1990): 130-67.

Glossary

For terms describing rhythm (*iambic, trochaic, dochmiac, choriambic / aeolic, anapaestic*) or the structure of song (*strophe, antistrophe, epode, triad, astrophic*), see the Metrical Appendix at the end of Chapter 2, pp. 34-5.

Aegospotamoi (battle of): Athenian catastrophe in 405 BC which decided the outcome of the Peloponnesian War (s.v.).

Aeschylus: tragic poet from Athens (*c.* 525-456 BC).

aidôs: 'shame', the sense of social propriety that prevents one from acting in a disapproved manner, and so encourages proper behaviour.

âkôn **homicide**: unintentional homicide, tried in the Palladion court; penalty was exile.

amoibaion: lyric (i.e. sung) exchange between character(s) and chorus.

Androtion: Athenian politician and antiquarian author (*c.* 410-340 BC).

Areopagus: 'Ares' hill' in Athens, where the Areopagus council met. Originally composed of aristocrats and so of tremendous political importance, the reduction of its earlier power was enacted (or confirmed) by the politician Ephialtes (462/1 BC) to competence in murder trials.

Aristophanes: comic poet from Athens (*c.* 460 to *c.* 368 BC).

âtê: 'delusion' (leading to) 'disaster'.

City Dionysia: pre-eminent festival for the performance of drama in Athens.

Colonus: a deme (s.v.) roughly one mile north-west of Athens; also the name of the deme's eponymous hero.

daimones: 'divine powers', term to be used for the power of the divine at various levels of specificity.

Decelea: a deme (s.v.) 20 km north-west of Athens, fortified by the Peloponnesians in 413 BC.

Delian League: name given to the alliance originally set up after the Persian Wars (490-479 BC), which became in practice the Athenian empire, dissolved at the end of the Peloponnesian War (s.v.).

Delphi: location of the oracle of Apollo, on the slopes of Mount Parnassus overlooking the Gulf of Corinth.

deme: territorial division, and basic constituent, of the Athenian political structure.

didascaliae: official lists recording details of theatrical performances in Athens, later collected by Aristotle (among others).

Eleusis: town 20 km west-north-west of Athens, site of the famous mystery cult of Demeter and Persephone.

episode: everything in the play between *stasima*.

Erechtheus: mythical king of Athens.

Glossary

Eumenides: ('Kindly Ones') another name for the Furies / Erinyes / *Semnai Theai*.

Euripides: tragic poet from Athens (*c.* 480 to *c.* 406 BC).

exodos: everything in the play after the last *stasimon* (s.v.).

Four Hundred: executive council, replacing the old *boulê*, established during the oligarchic revolution in 411 BC.

***hekôn* homicide**: intentional homicide, tried in the Areopagus court; penalties were death and property confiscation.

hero cult: worship of the powerful dead, especially the great figures of the epic past.

hippeis: the cavalry, second of the four property classes in Athens.

hypothesis: summary of play, with varying levels of production information, attached to the MSS, going back to the Hellenistic period (third-second centuries BC) and drawing at least partly on the *didascaliae* (s.v.).

Iophon: Sophocles' son, tragic poet.

kharis: 'favour', the fundamental element in the basic dynamic of reciprocity on the social, religious and institutional levels.

kommos: lyrical exchange between characters and chorus containing lamentation.

Life (of Sophocles): narrative of Sophocles' life, written in the Hellenistic period (third-second centuries BC) and transmitted with a range of his MSS.

liturgy: institution requiring the Athenian rich to pay for dramatic and dithyrambic performances (*khorêgia*) and the fitting out of a trireme.

Lysimachus: Greek grammarian and mythological author (second century BC).

Melos (sack of): Athenian reduction of the small island of Melos (415 BC) ended with the killing of the males and enslavement of the women and children.

miasma: ritual pollution, arising from killing, among other things.

Moriae: 'sacred olive trees' in Attica under the care of Zeus.

nomos: social norms ranging from 'custom' to 'written law'.

orchêstra: dancing area in the theatre in front of the acting area, where the chorus are positioned.

paiân: type of lyric song, usually celebrating victory.

parodos: chorus' entry song, after the *prologos* (s.v.), as it moves into the *orchêstra* (s.v.).

Pausanias: Greek antiquarian author (second century BC).

Peisander: Athenian politician, leading figure in the oligarchic revolution of 411 BC. On its failure, he left Athens and was condemned.

Peloponnesian War: conflict between the Spartans and their allies and the Delian League/ Athenian empire, which began in 431 BC and ended with Athenian defeat in 404 BC.

Pericles: Athenian politician at the start of the Peloponnesian War (*c.* 495-429 BC).

171

Glossary

philia: 'relationship with one's own', the term describes relationships within or outside the immediate family.

Pindar: lyric poet from Thebes (*c.* 518 to after 446 BC).

Plutarch: prolific Greek biographer and author (before 50 AD to after 120 AD).

Poseidon *Hippios*: Poseidon 'of horses', cult-title of the god at Colonus.

prologos: everything in the play preceding the chorus' entry song.

Samos (revolt of): attempt by this important island to secede from the Delian league (s.v.) (441-439 BC), crushed by Athens; Sophocles served as a general on this expedition.

Semnai Theai: 'Reverend Goddesses', another title for the Eumenides.

Sicily (expedition to): disastrous Athenian venture to conquer the island which ended in total defeat (415-413 BC).

skênê: wooden hut at the back of the acting area.

stasimon: a song (after the (s.v.) *parodos*) delivered by the chorus once it has taken position in the *orchêsta* (s.v.).

Thebes: chief city of Boeotia, region to the north-west of Athens; important enemy in the Peloponnesian War (s.v.)

Thirty Tyrants: oligarchic group who seized violent control of Athens in 404 BC after the end of the Peloponnesian War (s.v.), expelled in 403 BC before the democracy was restored.

xenos: 'guest' or 'host', participant in the institution / relationship of *xenia*, as well as 'stranger' or 'foreigner'.

Index

Index

Sophocles 12-13; suppliant
73-4, 75-9, 133; tomb 15-16,
21, 39-40, 42-4, 50, 67, 71,
78-80, 82-3, 110, 115, 123,
142-3n.12, 145n.27
olive(s) (*tree*) 68-70, 94-5,
99-100, 171
oracles 37-8, 39-41, 42, 45-6, 47,
54, 60-2, 65-8, 70, 77, 78, 85,
107, 120, 125, 127,
148nn.24&5

parricide 39, 56-7, 59, 65, 109,
145n.36, 147n.20, 147-8n.22,
148n.24
Pausanias 42, 69, 71, 95,
145n.27, 171
Peirithous 44, 81-2, 101-2, 114
Peloponnesian War 14-18, 19,
102-6, 171
Pericles 10-11, 20-1, 172
Persephone (*see also* 'Demeter')
81-2, 91, 94, 101, 114,
149n.18, 152n.15, 170
philia 58, 109, 126-7, 130-1,
150n.48, 156n.57, 172
Pindar 38, 42, 139n.14, 144n.15,
172
Plato 9, 23, 147n.20
politics (*and tragedy*) 14-18,
20-5
Polyneices 38-41, 46, 48-50, 59,
61-4, 67, 68, 70, 72, 74, 76,
78-9, 85, 88, 89, 96-7, 107-10,
115, 116, 118-21, 126, 128,
130-2, 135-6, 142n.10,
143n.13, 143n.4, 144n.22,
148n.24, 149n.13, 150n.46,
152n.16, 155n.29
pon- ('toil') 130
Poseidon 15, 20-1, 42, 68-9, 73,
93-5, 99-100, 103, 114,
119-20, 148nn.8&9, 149n.31,
154n.7, 172

purification (*see* 'Oedipus,
purification')

revolution (*oligarchic*; 411 BC)
11, 15, 20-1, 103, 105, 171

Samian War (441-39 BC) 9, 172
self-defence (*see also* 'homicide')
54, 55, 57-9, 147nn.13,20&21
Semnai Theai (*see also* 'Erinyes',
'Eumenides') 42-3, 71-2, 100,
132, 155n.39, 171, 172
skêptra kai thronoi ('sceptres
and thrones') 62-3, 128
smîkros logos ('small word') 62,
123, 130
Sicilian Expedition 11, 16, 105,
172
Sophocles *passim*:
autobiography (in the *OC*)
12-13, 20-1; and Colonus 10;
death 10, 12, 103, 145n.32;
generalship 9-10, 11; life and
career 9-14; piety 11-12;
plays: *Ajax* 12, 125, 145n.38,
151n.69 / *Antigone* 9-10, 42,
49-50, 135-7, 145n.32,
146nn.45-7 / *OT* 45-9, 53, 55,
59, 60, 67, 97-8, 135, 137,
143n.9, 145nn.32&34-5,
155n.35 / *OC passim* /
Philoctetes 12, 14-15, 16
suppliancy (*see also* 'Oedipus,
suppliant') 75-9, 106, 114,
118, 121-2, 128

Thebes (*see* Athens)
Theseus 22-3, 43-4, 46-9, 56, 61,
63-4, 68-71, 73-4, 76-81, 83-4,
88-91, 93, 96, 99-101, 103-5,
108, 109, 110-16, 117-18, 119,
120-1, 122, 123-4, 125-6, 128,
130, 132, 136, 139n.16,
142nn.10&12, 143nn.13&6,
145-6n.39, 148nn.24&7,

Index